# HELP!

# My Dog Doesn't Travel Well in the Car

Solving motion sickness
and other travelling issues

Toni Shelbourne

&

Karen Bush

## Other books by the authors

**HELP! My Dog is Scared of Fireworks**
Toni Shelbourne and Karen Bush
**HELP! My Dog is Destroying the Garden**
Toni Shelbourne and Karen Bush
**The Truth about Wolves and Dogs**
Toni Shelbourne *(Hubble & Hattie)*
**Among the Wolves: Memoirs of a Wolf Handler**
Toni Shelbourne *(Hubble & Hattie)*
**Dog-friendly Gardening**
Karen Bush *(Hubble & Hattie)*
**The Dog Expert**
Karen Bush *(Transworld)*
**The Difficult Horse**
Karen Bush and Sarah Fisher *(Crowood Press)*

ISBN-10: 1533481725
ISBN-13: 978-1533481726

**This book is dedicated to Mr P, Boris, Chester and Lisa - who have taught Toni and Karen so much about poor travellers!**

## ACKNOWLEDGMENTS

We are hugely grateful to all those who offered suggestions, and so generously shared their time and knowledge. We have done our best to ensure that the information contained within is, as far as we can ascertain, correct at time of writing: if there are any errors, then the fault is entirely ours, and not that of those who so kindly put up with our many queries!
Among those we would like to thank are:
Sarah Fisher, Robyn Hood, Mark Carpenter, Nick Thompson, Rachel Jackson, Dr Isla Fishburn, Amy Snow and Tallgrass Animal Acupressure Institute, Caroline Dalkin, Caroline Ingraham, Bob Atkins, James Sherman, Kate Hanley at f+w media, David & Charles

### Disclaimer

While the authors have made every attempt to offer accurate and reliable information to the best of their knowledge and belief, it is presented without any guarantee. The authors do not accept any responsibility in any manner whatsoever for any error or omission, or any loss, damage, injury, adverse outcome, or liability of any kind incurred as a result of the use of any of the information contained in this book, or reliance upon it. Please bear in mind that the advice in this book is not intended to replace veterinary attention. If in any doubt about any aspect of welfare, care and treatment, readers are advised to seek professional advice.

### About the cover image:

This delightful pose was taken in the farm yard one day while Meg was hanging out in the farm pick-up truck waiting for her farmer owner to take her back out to work with more sheep. She may look a little solemn here as she poses perfectly for Toni's camera, but in reality she is one happy collie!

**For simplicity, throughout this book, dogs have been referred to as 'he'**

# CONTENTS

# INTRODUCTION

You may consider your dog's problem to be impossible to solve, that 'he has always been this way' and therefore will continue to be so. We have both owned dogs that have struggled with a variety of travelling issues, and can reassure you that this is not the case!

Don't give up on your dog, as there is so much that can be done and if you are prepared to put in a little time and effort, travelling issues *can* be successfully overcome. In this book we aim to share our own personal experiences, so that you too can find ways in which you can help your four-legged passenger. Do remember that first of all though, you should get your dog checked out by your vet, just in case there are any health issues at the root of the problem.

We hope that you will find this book informative and of help to you and your dog, but if you feel at all uncertain about following any of the suggestions laid out in this book, then don't battle on alone, but seek the help of a qualified, reputable professional.

*Toni Shelbourne and Karen Bush*
*October 2016*

# 1
# THE POOR PASSENGER

You may not think of your dog's car travel issues as being anything more than annoying and certainly not as life-threatening, but the fact is that they can be: anything which interferes with the driver's ability to concentrate is hazardous and has potential to contribute to, or directly cause, an accident.

Apart from safety aspects, if you have ever suffered from travel issues yourself, then you will understand just how miserable they can make your pet. If you have never experienced any such problems, then you have been fortunate, but take our word for it that it can be pretty grim! And it is not just your dog who suffers if he finds car travel difficult; even the shortest of trips can become an ordeal for everyone else in the vehicle too. It can also end up limiting your activities together - the amount of preparation needed for a journey may rule out any spur-of-the-moment fun outings, while if you are planning special days out or considering going on holiday, you may think twice about taking him along too. That's not all: should a trip to the vets be necessary, the journey to the surgery can massively increase the stress of the visit for both of you. And if you have another dog, there is also the possibility that he may pick up on, or be stressed by the behaviour of his companion – and the only thing worse than one poor traveller in the car is two!

When dealing with travelling issues of any kind, finding a solution is not always straightforward, as there may be more than one underlying cause which needs to be addressed. A dog which vomits, for example, may indeed be suffering from motion sickness – but there may also be physical imbalance and lack of co-ordination, an inner ear problem, poor driving, stress-related issues, or even anticipatory anxiety following unpleasant experiences during early car rides all contributing to the problem. Careful observation, sensible management as well as actively working to improve matters, and very often a multi-pronged approach may therefore be called for. Try to be open-minded and prepared to look into a wide range of possible underlying causes, even if at first you are inclined to dismiss them as being of no consequence.

This might sound like a lot of work and already you may find yourself wondering if it is worth sorting? Well, yes, because learning to live with car travelling issues does no-one any favours. Your dog would thank you for it if he could, and when you rediscover the pleasure of going out in the car with a confident, happy passenger, you will be glad that you made the effort.

You will find that a lot of this book deals with Tellington TTouch: it plays a large and indispensable part in our own lives, and we have found it to be in-valuable in offering a variety of ways in which you can help your dog overcome any travelling issues. It is also simple to learn and easy to do! It is not the only modality which may be of benefit to your dog however, so we have also included details of those others which are most commonly used and which we have found helpful. They can be utilised on their own, or many can be combined with each other as well as with TTouch to good effect.

It is always important to remember that every dog is an individual, and that what works well for one may be less successful with another. This is not due to the problem being impossible to solve, or to a chosen remedy or course of action being invalid, but rather merely points to the need to explore more than one avenue. Do bear in mind too, that sometimes it is necessary to be patient and give something sufficient time in which to work.

## Spotting the warning signs

In this book we'll be taking a look at those issues which mostly commonly cause problems when travelling, including anxiety, jumping around in the car, reacting to outside stimuli and motion sickness.

The sort of behaviours which may tell you that your dog isn't very happy about being in the car can range from mild to extreme. While some are pretty obvious such as vomiting or barking, other indications may be more low-key, such as panting or lip-licking. Do take notice of these more subtle indicators as it is often easier to resolve problems if you take action at an early stage than if you wait until they have escalated. Your dog's behaviours can also help to provide clues to underlying causes, and help you to decide on the best course of action to take.

Tell-tale signs to be aware of can include a whole variety of behaviours, such as:

- whining
- drooling
- inactivity, listlessness
- freezing into one position
- scratching at the car interior
- restlessness, constantly changing position
- jumping around
- destructiveness – tearing at the car interior or chewing bedding
- vomiting
- diarrhoea/urination
- vocalizing – whining, yapping, barking, howling, moaning
- reluctance or refusal to get in the car
- yawning
- panting, lip-licking
- refusing to lie down
- wanting to be close to you
- shaking, trembling
- reactivity to movement outside the car such as dogs, people, cyclists, bikers and other cars

As well as watching out for any of these indicators, observe your dog's general posture and also his facial expressions, since just as with humans, these can speak volumes about the way he is feeling and the nature of his travelling issues.

# 2
# CAUSE AND EFFECT

All sorts of issues can contribute towards your dog being a less than happy passenger in the car, but if you can work out what these are, then it will be easier for you to determine the best course of action to take. The underlying cause may be something relatively simple and obvious or might be more obscure, requiring you to be a bit of a detective, exercising good powers of observation, a degree of empathy, resourcefulness and being prepared to keep an open mind. Sometimes there will be more than one issue which needs addressing, and in some cases you may find that a certain amount of trial-and-error experimentation is called for, such as in finding the best travelling position in the car for your dog.

The following issues are all commonly associated with travelling problems, and are well worth investigating:

## Health issues
Certain health issues such as vestibular disease and middle or inner ear infections may cause difficulty in balancing and predispose to nausea, while a reluctance to get in the car might be due to apprehension of the journey, but could also be due to a physical inability to

jump in. Although arthritis is most often associated with senior dogs, it is not a condition confined solely to the elderly, so shouldn't be discounted on grounds of age: perhaps hip or elbow dysplasia is present, or there is a cruciate ligament problem in the hind legs: or maybe rapid growth in a youngster could be causing difficulties. There are any number of conditions that may be causing pain, which will be further intensified by the constant movement of the car, and can lead to problems in balancing.

*Always* consult your vet if you suspect that a health issue could be a contributory factor in travelling issues: and do not be too quick to dismiss physical pain as an underlying cause just because you haven't spotted any obvious indications. It doesn't mean that discomfort isn't present as dogs can be incredibly stoic and very good at concealing it, so it can be a good idea to make an appointment anyway to at least eliminate it as being a cause. This will also give you the opportunity to discuss any remedies or medications you would like to try.

**Comfort**

What you may perceive as being comfortable isn't necessarily so from your dog's point of view. Seats aren't always wide enough to accommodate him in the position he feels happiest in; and just as some people feel nauseous when in vehicles where they are sitting sideways-on to the movement, but feel fine when facing forwards, the same may apply to your four legged passenger. Soft suspension can also lead to motion sickness or make it difficult for your dog to balance himself.

He may also find it hard to balance or to find a

position which is comfortable if his movement is restricted by a crate which is too small or by an incorrectly adjusted seatbelt. It is also important to consider any bedding you provide for him to lie on – if it slides around as you travel it can be very unnerving. Good rubber matting is not only easy to clean in the event of any little accidents, but will provide better grip for paws; and if you provide a bed, select one with a non-slip underside to help with this issue.

**Balance**
Difficulty in balancing can lead to apprehension (and injury) and may be an issue even if your dog is lying down. Rather than trying to remain still, some dogs will actually become more restless in an attempt to find their 'car legs' making things worse rather than better. Poor balance isn't just something which affects stiff, less mobile senior dogs, or one which has an injury, but can be an issue present right from early puppyhood. Like human toddlers, as puppies grow they can become physically out of balance as their bodies change shape and size – you may notice a lack of co-ordination and clumsiness at times. Add a moving vehicle into the equation, and the result will be an even greater difficulty in balancing. While many dogs do grow out of it by the time they have achieved full growth, some individuals continue to struggle with physical balance as adults; and others may develop negative associations with the car as a result of their early unpleasant experiences.

Balance issues can also be an indication of certain health problems, so ask your vet to check your dog to ensure there is nothing more serious going on. Once this is eliminated, you can help improve your dog's balance and teach him how to deal with the motion of the car through use of exercises such as the Tellington TTouch Confidence Course, explained later in this book.

## Motion sickness

Motion sickness can be the most miserable experience as anyone will know who has ever suffered from it themselves. Some dogs suffer really badly from motion sickness, even on the very shortest of trips, and it can lead to vomiting and will increase feelings of anxiety and create disagreeable associations with travelling.

It is most common in puppies and young dogs, possibly because the structures in the ear which help with balance aren't yet fully developed, and many will simply 'grow out of it'. But just as with humans, there are many who don't - an estimated one in four - and even if it does pass with maturity, it can create and reinforce lifelong negative associations with being in the car. Bear in mind that your dog may be experiencing motion sickness even if he doesn't actually vomit; and that vomiting (and also loss of bladder or bowel control) can be due to stress and apprehension as well as to motion sickness. Because it is frequently linked to poor balance (see above) improving your dog's posture through activities such as the Tellington TTouch Confidence Course can often produce a massive improvement.

## Digestive upset

It may seem odd, but don't rule out diet or food intolerances as a possible contributory cause; travelling problems can sometimes be linked to underlying digestive disturbances. It may be worth trying a different diet or adding probiotics to aid digestion.

## Canine sensitivity

Dogs are far more sensitive than us to a wide range of sensations and things we don't notice ourselves or take for granted can make life unpleasant or even scary for them - for example, the vibration of car roof rails at certain speeds. Cars are also so well-made these days that pressure changes in the ears caused when the door is slammed can cause discomfort and may trigger fear. Other noises, such as vehicle reversing sensors, heavy rain drumming on the roof - even the click of indicators or swipe of windscreen wipers - can prove hard to tolerate for some dogs, especially those which are noise sensitive anyway.

Keeping a diary can be helpful in trying to pinpoint possible problem areas and may give you ideas as to things to change or try doing differently: note down what was going on when behaviours are triggered or increase or decrease in intensity.

## Stress

Dogs which fly from side to side of the car with tails wagging, and probably barking loudly at the same time aren't necessarily happy and excited, but are more likely to be stressed and nervous; they aren't relaxed and comfortable enough in their bodies or minds to settle quietly.

Although you may consider the car to be a safely enclosed, rather boring environment it can seem anything but that for your pet. There are unfamiliar noises going on both within the car and outside it, while the combined movement of the vehicle and stimulation of looking out of the window and seeing things whizzing past outside exacerbates things even further; for some, even the different smell of the interior may cause concern.

If you become cross with the actions of other motorists, even though your annoyance is not directed towards your dog, it can cause stress levels to rise even further, so trying to remain calm at all times is important; this will also of course, ensure that your driving skills are better! There are occasions when it can be difficult, but try not to react to any stressed behaviour which your dog exhibits, and note any possible triggers. Dogs are highly sensitive to charged, emotional atmospheres, and while you may not always be able to pre-empt an issue, you *can* take steps to avoid making it worse.

**Reactive**
Dogs which tend to be reactive will also find it hard to lie down quietly in the car. Where a dog is aggressive-reactive it is essential to seek experienced professional one-to-one help as soon as possible. When in the car, take steps to ensure the safety of all other occupants, since if travelling with another dog he may redirect his frustration on to his companion, or even onto humans if they try to interrupt the behaviour. When taking him to and from the car, make sure he is wearing a leash, and if necessary put a muzzle on him if there is any risk, however small, of undesirable behaviours being triggered – for example by other passing dogs, joggers, postmen, cyclists etc. It may seem excessive, and your dog may be acting defensively, out of fear rather than nastiness, but others may not be sympathetic, and in this litigious day and age you cannot be too careful.

**Associations**
Bad experiences can lead to even the calmest of dogs

becoming anxious – for example if he has been involved in an accident, abandoned or stolen from a car, had frequent trips to visit the vet, or experienced a traumatic event such as his tail being accidentally shut in the door.

Accompanying another dog which is a stressed passenger can also result in both dogs developing travelling issues. It can sometimes take a long time to overcome any memories of past bad experiences triggered by being in the car, but these fears will need to be addressed for your dog to become a confident traveller again.

Bear in mind that the first car journey your puppy ever takes is very often the one where you collect him to bring him home – for you an exciting experience, but quite possibly less so from your puppy's point of view. He is being removed from the security and familiarity of the only home and family he has ever known; he may feel nauseous during the journey, adding to the poor association, and his first few successive trips thereafter may be to the vets where he is handled by strangers, has uncomfortable vaccinations, and is in an environment where there may be other stressed dogs.

It doesn't make for a great start and not surprisingly he may in future associate trips in the car with unpleasant things happening! You'll find some advice and tips on how to make your new puppy's first car trip as pleasant and stress-free as possible later on in this book, and it is well worth making the effort as you'll be helping to set the pattern for the rest of his life.

Of course, not all associations with the car may be nasty ones but can still lead to problems; if you most often use it to take him to places where he goes for a walk for example, then he may bark and jump around in the car through excitement, impatience and frustration (or a combination of these) due to the fun he anticipates on reaching his destination.

# 3
# GIVING YOUR DOG A GOOD RIDE

Solving some travelling issues may be as simple as ensuring that you are giving your dog a good ride … of course, there may be more involved, but it is still an important aspect which can contribute to problems, so it is worth giving your usual arrangements some consideration.

## Access
If your dog is reluctant to get in the car due to lack of confidence, anxiety, or fear-related issues, then forcibly picking him up and putting him inside will not make matters any better and could actually make them worse. Your actions might cause him to behave defensively, and will certainly damage any trust between you. Put yourself in a similar position – for example, if you are scared of spiders, then having someone tell you not to be so silly and compelling you to touch one will not change your attitude towards them, no matter how unfounded and irrational your fears may be! So do respect your dog's feelings; it can often be all too easy for us to override them, sometimes without even realising this is happening. Remember that what is easy and most convenient for us is not always so for your dog and may overlook his emotional and physical state

and needs. In such cases, we suggest that you go right back to scratch and take the time to build up his confidence in small, easy steps: you'll find advice on how to do this in the section on travel training, and it pays dividends both in helping him to be a willing, happier and more co-operative passenger and in retaining his trust and friendship.

Getting into the car may be physically difficult and can cause discomfort for some dogs; where the issue is one of mobility then picking him up and placing him inside the car would seem the obvious solution. Many dogs do, however, dislike being picked up, and if he has health issues it may be painful for him. With larger dogs, or if you have a bad back, then picking him up may not be a viable option anyway! Whatever the size, your dog may prefer it if you allow him to load himself by walking up a ramp; on reaching your destination, he will then also be able to get out with no painful jarring of his legs.

It is possible to buy ramps, or if you are handy at DIY you could make your own – but it must be suitable for both you, your car, and your dog. It should be light enough for you to carry and set up easily, but sturdy enough to be stable. It is essential that it is wide enough for him to walk up, since if it is too narrow he may misstep, which may damage his confidence even if he doesn't actually fall off. It should have a grippy surface, as much for the assurance that this will give him as from the point of view of safety. Length is also important, since a very short ramp is also likely to be a steep one, and your dog may struggle to cope with the gradient. This means that it may need to fold or hinge in some way to enable you to fit it into the car, so you can take it with you and use it again at your destination.

*(photo: Toni Shelbourne)*

Don't expect your dog to understand immediately how to use a ramp; introduce it gradually – it is something which you could include as part of the Tellington TTouch Method Confidence Course explained later on in this book. Begin with it lying flat on the ground, encouraging him to walk slowly along it so he is in a good balanced state and has time to think

*(photo: Toni Shelbourne)*

about where he is placing his feet.

Once he is confident doing this, raise one end slightly using a curb, garden step, low wall or similar, Remember that as it becomes higher he must be able to walk off the end onto something – don't ask him to try and turn around while on the ramp. Practice walking both up and down the gradient formed, and gradually increase the height.

When you feel ready to try using it with the car, make sure your dog has a straight approach. Attempting to get on from the side if you haven't left quite enough room, can be very challenging for some dogs with mobility problems, and even if he is able-bodied, he may find it hard to accurately judge foot placement and to align himself along it, increasing the risk of him falling off. It can be a good idea to pop a harness on him, as this will make it easier for you to assist and support him if necessary.

## In the car
### *Windows and doors*
Good ventilation is really important for anyone who suffers from motion sickness, and no less so for your dog - a bit of fresh air can often do a lot to help reduce feelings of nausea. Open a rear window a little, although not so much that he can put his head out. This could result in grit and debris getting into his eyes or could lead to injury; and might also be a dangerous distraction for other motorists. There is a risk too, that if opened too wide it might be viewed as an escape route. Various products can be bought from motoring shops and online, such as expanding grilles and window socks which will make the opening secure and allow you to have the window open a little wider.

Cars are so well made these days that the change in pressure as doors are shut can be physically unpleasant and for some dogs may be a frightening sensation; leaving a window partially open before shutting the last door or loading your dog will avoid this. Switching on fans to heat or cool the interior more quickly can also produce changes in pressure. Don't forget to shut doors slowly and quietly (making sure first that tails are safely inside) and check that they are completely closed. If your dog is travelling loose in the back of the car, put the child locks on so that the doors cannot be accidentally opened if he paws or scrabbles at the interior.

If your dog is contained within the car by a seat belt or in a crate, check that he does not become chilled by cool air blowing directly over him from a window, as he will be unable to move away from it. Exterior noise from other vehicles, especially on motorways, can also sound very loud when a window is open, so avoid positioning him right next to it.

Sun shades for windows are also essential bits of kit, ensuring that your dog is not constantly trapped in the sun – they can also usefully reduce the amount of visual stimulus which may excite or lead to nausea. Shades come in all shapes and sizes with various ways of attaching them; but if you find that your dog continually knocks them off, try using window socks or adhesive window tint, available from high street automobile stores and online. Do not tint front side windows which in order to remain legal must allow 70% plus of VLT (visible light transmission).

Avoid taking your dog out in the car in hot weather, as dogs find it much harder to cope with high temperatures than we do, and it will all add to his discomfort. Don't assume that switching on the air conditioning is the answer, as it can take a while to reduce the temperature inside the car to a comfortable level. It can also make a noise while running which may be upsetting to your dog, and requires that you keep all the windows closed, thereby removing the beneficial fresh-air element.

### *Try a different position*
Seats in cars are designed with humans in mind rather than canine passengers, so if your dog travels sitting on a back seat he may find it awkward, limiting his position. Many dogs dislike lying sideways to the direction of travel, but larger ones will have little option, and even small dogs often find it cramped and difficult to prevent their front paws from sliding off the edge. Try filling in the space in the footwell to give more room and choice about how he is positioned. Using a hammock-style cover will protect car seat upholstery and eliminates the danger of your dog falling off the seat - but still fill in the footwell space anyway, to give a more stable feel beneath his feet. Make sure that any covers are securely fitted so they do not slide around when your dog jumps into and out of the car.

If your dog is contained within a crate or by a seatbelt, experiment with its position; the centre of the car is usually the most stable place where he will experience the least amount of sideways swing when you are manoeuvring or driving round bends – folding the rear seats down if this is possible may help. Another reason for trying a central position is that he is less likely to be disturbed there by any noise or vibration from the wheels. If he is near to a door with speakers, the same may also apply if you have the radio or music playing.

It is not advisable to travel your dog in the rear cargo section; the space is designed to accommodate shopping and luggage, rather than to meet the requirements of a dog. He may feel cramped and be unable to position himself comfortably, while the side windows in the area won't open so that ventilation and air flow is likely to be poor. Some dogs may also feel distressed at being kept at such a distance from you. More importantly, the consequences for him in the event of a rear collision could be fatal.

### *Mirrors*

Sometimes anxiety can be created by things that never occur to us, such as the reflection of your eyes in the driving mirror alarming your dog in the back, who just sees a pair of staring disembodied eyes! Simply changing the angle of the mirror can solve this particular issue, and it's a useful reminder that sometimes it can be helpful to quite literally put yourself in your dog's place. Just as you might get down on all fours to get a dog's eye perspective when puppy-proofing your house and looking for potential hazards, try sitting in your dog's place in the car to get a feel for anything which may be contributing to his travelling issues.

### *Smellies*

Get rid of any air fresheners; especially when new they can be overwhelming to our own noses – imagine how much more intense they must seem to your dog, with his far superior and ultra-sensitive sense of smell. If you smoke, avoid doing so when in the car as apart from the health issues for human and doggy passengers, tobacco smoke can make the symptoms of motion sickness worse. Even if no-one else is in the car, remember that the odour of cigarette smoke can linger long afterwards.

### *Static strips*

Some cars seem to pick up a lot of static which can adversely affect your dog. If he receives a shock it can be unpleasant and possibly even frightening for him, and a build-up of static is thought by some to contribute to feelings of nausea. There is much debate over whether fitting an anti-static earthing strip is of any benefit, but it does no harm to try - they are readily available from motoring stores and online, and cost very little.

### *Try a different car*

Various cars give different rides; in estate cars for example, your dog may experience more sideways swing, while other vehicles may have harder or softer suspension which can affect the ride he gets for better or worse.

At certain speeds there may also be noises which disturb your dog, caused by vibrations in the car, from roof rails or grit trapped in tyre treads, or from road surfaces. They may be subtle or even undetectable to us, but picked by your pet.

It can be worth trying him in a different car to see if there is any improvement, and which may help in identifying problem areas. Try asking relatives and friends if they would mind chauffeuring you with your dog for a few short trips, or hire a car – but make sure you take steps to protect interiors if your dog is liable to vomiting!

## Take a break

On longer trips, allow time in your schedule for taking a break, stopping somewhere every one and a half to two hours so that you can let your dog out to stretch his legs and have a pee. Travelling is never restful, and even while lying down, he will still be constantly balancing himself; and if contained in a crate or with a seatbelt his movement will be limited, and he may become stiff and uncomfortable. It will also give him the opportunity to have a drink; some dogs won't touch anything while in the car, even when it is stationary. Breaks are good for the driver too!

If taking your car on a boat or ferry, check the operator's regulations: some insist that dogs remain in the car – in which case stay with him – but if he is allowed to accompany you, he may be better in the fresh air above than below decks.

## Improve your driving

It sounds like very obvious advice but is so often the last thing considered; sometimes it is our own driving skills (or lack of them) which are responsible for turning our dogs into poor passengers. Drive carefully and smoothly; reading the road ahead is of course essential for safety, but will also have a direct bearing on the ride you give your dog as he won't be able anticipate any sudden braking, rapid acceleration or sharp turns. He may also become stressed by rough gear changes or if you start shouting at other motorists!

## Stay calm

Your dog's behaviour in the car may be putting a strain on your patience, but whatever he is doing, it is really important to try and remain as calm and neutral as possible; dogs are very observant of, and sensitive to, your tone of voice and body language. Should you shout, or exclaim, or even just mutter in annoyance at his actions, it can make matters worse and will certainly reinforce any anxieties he has. Take a deep breath and let it out as slowly as possible!

Careless pedestrians, thoughtless cyclists, and inconsiderate motorists, getting stuck in a traffic jam, or being late for an appointment can also conspire to raise your blood pressure and lead to an ill-judged outburst which can stress your dog. While you cannot change the actions of other road users, you can control your own responses, although it may not always be easy. It is however, something to strive for, which will make your driving safer and benefit your dog, who will take his cue from you. At any time when you are feeling stressed, you may find that the following breathing exercise helps you to maintain a measure of equilibrium:

### *Breathing stress-buster*

Any time you are feeling anxious and under stress can have an effect on your breathing, which may become more rapid and shallow. Restoring a slower, deeper manner of breathing will help you to relax and be calmer and more co-ordinated in your movements and is a great stress-buster. It is quite possible that your dog will note the change in your breathing pattern, producing a beneficial effect on him. Practice it at home first, with no distractions.

1. Sit in a chair and place one hand on your abdomen, just above your belly-button.
2. Breathe in deeply through your nose, counting to ten as you do so. Let the breath move your hand outwards.

3.  Hold your breath for a count of five – but without pressing your lips tightly together. Think instead about your diaphragm helping to contain the air within your lungs.
4.  Release your breath, but not all at once: allow it to move out between slightly parted lips over a count of ten.
5.  Repeat five times.
6.  Once you are familiar with the exercise, try it while driving, but without placing your hand on your abdomen.

## Containment

In some countries, you are legally required to contain your dog in some way while in the car: but even where this is not the case it is generally a sensible measure to take. It will help to prevent him from interfering with the driver, or from causing injury to other passengers in the event of a collision, when it is possible for a dog travelling loose to be thrown forwards with potentially killing force.

An effective method of containment may also prevent your dog from escaping and getting loose on the carriageway should you be involved in an accident. In addition, if you have several dogs travelling together in the car, keeping them separately confined can be useful in keeping them from physically annoying, or redirecting any reactive behaviours onto each other.

There are various ways in which you can contain your dog. Each have plus and minus points, and none are absolutely perfect. You should however, be aware that some systems and designs are better than others at protecting your dog from injury, and we would strongly recommend that you research your choices carefully with this in mind; you will find plenty of information on this aspect available online.

The way in which you choose to contain your dog can also affect the ride he has, and therefore how well and confidently he travels.

### Dog guards:
Made of mesh and/or tubular steel, these will allow your dog the maximum amount of freedom of movement, enabling him to find the position which suits him best.

This freedom will of course, also allow him to jump around in the car. If not very securely fixed they can be pulled down, which can cause fright. There have also been instances of dogs biting at, and succeeding in actually crushing and distorting the tubular sections of cheaper products.

### Seatbelts:
Doggy seatbelts will keep your dog confined to one area of the car, but some dogs may find this limitation of movement stressful, and may even panic. A seatbelt should be introduced slowly and in careful stages, even if he is already accustomed to wearing a harness when out on leash walks.

If he is unused to a harness, then Tellington TTouch body wraps (explained later in this book) can be a good way of initially familiarising your dog with the feel.

Do carefully check all seatbelt adjustments, and if your dog moves around, keep an eye on him to ensure that he does not become entangled in it.

### Crate:
Travelling in a crate can encourage your dog to lie down, and will prevent him from being able to jump

about in the car or interfering with other dogs travelling with him. If he is reactive it can, if necessary, be covered with a sheet to stop him from becoming visually stimulated by passing vehicles and other objects he spots through the window. While many dogs feel safer travelling in a covered 'den', some may become anxious if they cannot see you, so you may need to arrange things so that he is able to keep you in sight.

Crates come in all shapes and sizes including square, rectangular and tubular, and are made of a variety of materials including steel mesh, fabric and plastic. Rigid plastic travelling kennels tend to be more enclosed and may be a better option for dogs which tend to be destructive, as it may reduce the risk of injury (or escape) if he bites or scratches at the sides.

Whatever type of crate you select, it must however, be large enough to allow your dog to stand up, lie down and comfortably turn around. Crates and kennels should be secured using seatbelts or rock-climbing carabineers to attach them to fixed inner fittings so they will not slide around, or in the case of smaller ones, fall off seats into the footwell.

### Introducing a crate

You should introduce the crate in your home first, where your dog will feel most relaxed and confident. If he is already accustomed to regularly using a crate indoors, do not assume that he will automatically accept it when it is placed in the car though; although you may be able to skip the 'at home' step, you should repeat the introductory procedure with it in the vehicle.

Set up the crate indoors with some comfy bedding inside, feed him his meals in there and pop toys and treats in for him to discover. This will encourage him to use it, and make it an inviting place with pleasant associations where he will voluntarily choose to spend time relaxing. Never try and manhandle him inside, no matter how gentle you are about it! You can however, introduce a verbal cue 'Crate!' or similar whenever you spot him going into it, so that you can ask him to go in on those occasions when you want him to. Tossing a treat in there for him to eat will enable you to repeat and establish this process more quickly. Leave the door open at all times initially, so he can come and go as he wishes; only when he is happy to voluntarily spend time in there should you shut the door. This should be for just a minute or two at first; provide a long-lasting treat such as a tightly stuffed Kong, or choose a time of day when he normally enjoys a nap so he is less likely to be concerned about it. Gradually you can increase the time you leave the door shut; how quickly you progress depends on how quickly he takes to the crate. Most dogs do enjoy 'denning' especially if the crate is covered, as it provides them with a private, quiet space where they can feel safe. Do not abuse this though, and never leave your dog crated for more than two hours, and never unattended during the introductory process.

Once your dog is completely happy about being in the crate in your house you can begin to introduce it in the car in much the same way – although never leave your dog on his own in the car, or practice this part of his car training in warm weather in case of overheating.

## Travelling tips

**DO** make sure that your dog wears a collar and tag with your contact details on it, even if you are only going on the shortest of training trips and don't intend to take him out of the car between leaving and returning home. It is a legal requirement when out in public – and that includes when he is in your car out on a public highway. Should the worst happen and he somehow manages to escape while putting him in or taking him out of the car, it will also make it easier for someone to catch hold of him, and because collar ID is quick and easy to check, could help you to be more speedily reunited.

**DO** load and unload your dog into the car from the kerbside when using side doors. This will be safer for you and your dog, and as passing vehicles and cyclists will also be less visible they will be less likely to frighten, or to trigger a reactive response.

**DO** put a leash on your dog before letting him out of the car, and make sure that you have hold of it properly before letting him out – especially if he is a nervous passenger and keen to make a quick exit. Even if he is brilliantly behaved, this is still a necessity as legally it is an offence for him to be on a designated road without being held on a leash. Local authorities may have similar byelaws covering public areas such as car parks.

**DO** teach a really solid 'wait' command so that your dog learns to wait for you to invite him to jump into or out of the car. If he takes a hasty or unexpected leap he may be unbalanced and land awkwardly or risk injury if, for example, you haven't got the door fully opened. This will do little to change any concerns he already has, and may create additional ones.

**DO** provide water. Travelling can be thirsty work for calm dogs, while if your dog pants a lot or vomits he may become dehydrated. Place a non-spill water bowl where he can reach it: or if he is reluctant to drink while on the move, offer him a drink whenever you stop.

**DON'T** position your dog next to airbags in the car unless they have been disabled, as they could seriously injure or even kill him should they go off.

**DON'T** travel your dog on the rear window shelf of your car as this can interfere with the driver's view and may distract any motorists behind. Bear in mind that the area of the vehicle behind the rear passenger seats is most liable to damage in the event of a rear collision.

**DON'T** leave your dog unattended in the car. Most of us are familiar with the 'hot cars kill' warnings each summer, but even mild weather can lead to interior temperatures and humidity levels rapidly becoming dangerously high. Don't assume that leaving the air conditioning on will solve the problem, as there have been numerous instances of it failing, with tragic consequences. There is also a very real danger of him becoming a victim of theft, whether intentionally targeted, or indirectly if the car is stolen, with him becoming an unwilling passenger.

Another very good reason for never leaving your dog alone in the car is that he may be disturbed by passers-by; some may stop to look at him through the window, may tease him or perhaps push their fingers (or other objects) through gaps in the window. Even if your dog is normally friendly towards people, it may be a different matter when he is in the car, as he may feel threatened and cornered, leading to him reacting defensively or aggressively and possibly falling foul of the Dangerous Dogs Act as a result. Apart from the issues of welfare and safety, any of these occurrences are likely to further confirm any anxieties your dog may have about being in the car.

One last point worth considering is that a heavy rain shower or hail storm can produce a lot of noise on the metal skin of a car, which can be very frightening for your dog, especially if he is noise sensitive. If you (or someone he knows and trusts) are with him, then steps can at least be taken to reassure him and minimise any distress.

# 4
# FINDING A SOLUTION

Your dog cannot help it if he isn't the greatest passenger to have in the car with you – but you don't have to learn to live with it, as there is plenty you can do to improve the situation. It may be possible to help him to completely overcome any travelling issues he has, but even if this doesn't prove feasible, you will at least be able to make trips a lot more pleasant and less stressful for you both.

Don't be tempted to put things off in the hope that he might 'grow out of it', because there is a very good chance that he won't, and the longer you leave things, the more established any negative associations with being in the car will become. Even if your dog currently shows only a very mild level of concern about travelling, it is advisable to take action before it escalates and what started as a minor inconvenience becomes a challenging issue that may be more difficult to resolve.

Some issues may be deeply seated and will require a long-term approach. It may also be necessary to adopt several of the suggestions offered in the following pages, rather than relying on just a single one. Sometimes there is more than one underlying issue, and the resolution of one reveals another beneath:

this process has been likened to peeling the layers of an onion, with each needing to be removed before finally reaching the central core.

While working through the issues your dog has, it is okay to be soothing, offering comfort and reassurance as appropriate; this will not reinforce any fears or anxieties he has but *can* do a lot to help him feel safe and less stressed. You should however, be careful of your personal safety and that of others at all times: always bear in mind that a frightened or wildly over-excited dog may lack self-control and behave out of his normal character.

Never attempt to force him to face up to anything that frightens him, as you'll lose his trust, and he'll just become more frightened. Above all, no matter how trying things may be for you, remember that it is probably much, much worse for your pet. If there are occasions when you find your patience being severely tested, then take a break as any loss of temper on your part is also likely to set him back as well as damaging bonds of trust.

Some of the suggestions in this book will demand commitment, time and effort on your part, but it will all have been worth it when you reach your goal of making outings in the car an event to enjoy rather than endured or even feared.

### Health check

A health check should *always* be the starting place when trying to resolve any issues your dog has, even where these appear to be psychological in nature. Emotional and behavioural problems often stem from physical issues and each can exert a strong influence on the other.

Before pursuing any of the suggestions outlined in this book, your vet's surgery should therefore be your first port of call: make an appointment to have your dog thoroughly checked over for any health issues. If physical problems are discovered, these can then be treated, and if required, any physiotherapy arranged; in some cases this may prove sufficient to settle the travelling issue without further action being necessary.

**Finding help**
Should your dog be severely phobic about being in the car, or if you find it difficult to cope by yourself, or simply feel that you would like to have some expert hands-on assistance, we recommend that following a vet check, you seek help from an animal behaviour counsellor or a Tellington TTouch Companion Animal practitioner, on referral from your vet.

Be aware that the breadth and depth of knowledge and practical experience of those who advertise their services as 'counsellors' or 'trainers' can be variable; anyone can give themselves these titles and even if someone has good credentials on paper, may lack hands-on skills. Check them out very carefully and thoroughly before enlisting their services, satisfying yourself that anyone you consult works in a humane and compassionate manner, using only positive training methods.

You will find some helpful information on what to look for and how to find someone in your area who may be able to help on the Association of Pet Dog Trainers (APDT) website. Contact details for the APDT, Association of Pet Behaviour Counsellors (APBC) and Tellington TTouch Practitioners can be found at the end of this book.

## ADAPTIL

Adaptil (previously known as DAP) is a synthetic copy of a natural canine pheromone produced by nursing bitches which helps to comfort and reassure their puppies. It can also help adult dogs, promoting calmness and reducing anxiety during times of stress. It is colourless and odourless, with no sedative effect and can be safely used alongside medications to help your dog feel safe and secure.

It is available from vets, pet shops and online in the form of impregnated collars, reusable diffusers (similar to air freshener devices) and as a spray. The diffuser is plugged into an electrical socket and left continuously running in the room in your house where your dog spends the majority of his time. It covers up to 50-70 square metres, and will last for around 4 weeks; refill vials can be bought and replaced as needed.

Using Adaptil in the house will mean that when you begin travel training, its benefits will already be in place. The action of the diffuser can then be further reinforced by applying the Adaptil spray to the bedding in the car. Allow 15 minutes between spraying any objects and allowing your dog to use them: its effect will last for around 2-3 hours. Adaptil also produce non-pheromone based tablets which should be given two hours before travelling – see also Calming Products.

## CHANGING THE ASSOCIATIONS

Try to create pleasant associations with being in the car, such as encouraging your dog to hop in while it's stationary and offering him a really tasty treat, maybe even feeding him his meals in there, or perhaps having a little game with his favourite toy.

If your dog tends to get over-excited about going for a ride in the car, then as well as creating nice associations, you might want to give some thought to creating different ones such as lying or sitting quietly while you do some soothing Tellington TTouches: or chewing a long lasting treat such as a tightly stuffed Kong, which can be a de-stressing activity. You could also take him regularly for 'boring' journeys where he doesn't go for exciting free-running exercise at the end; it might even be just a short drive around the block and back home again without ever getting out!

You might also teach your dog to settle in the car using clicker training or other positive markers for lying down and being calm. It can often take time to change your dog's expectations, so be prepared to be patient. Remember too, that hyperactive behaviours are sometimes due to stress rather than enthusiasm. It can be easy to mistake one for the other, so observe your dog carefully - enlist the help of an experienced animal behaviourist, trainer or TTouch Practitioner if you aren't sure.

## FOOD AND WATER

Don't feed your dog just before travelling - but don't starve him either as although he may bring up less, it won't stop him from vomiting if he suffers from motion sickness. Missing out on a meal can also cause stress vomiting in some dogs. If he is due for a meal, do however, give it to him at least three to four hours before your journey, and make it a small, light and easily digested meal rather than a large, heavy one. If your dog tends to be excitable or reactive, it is worth considering what you feed him; changing over to a more natural, additive free diet often sees a sometimes dramatic improvement in behaviour. This also extends to treats if you use them as a part of your travel-training; stick to ones which are natural and free from artificial additives and preservatives.

Many therapeutic benefits are claimed for ginger, and it is of course, a traditional remedy for motion sickness related nausea in humans; many people swear by it for dogs too. Although a pre-journey ginger biscuit is unlikely to do any harm and may be worth trying, do not give ginger tablets, powder, extract, raw ginger, or ginger in any other form to your dog without first consulting your vet as an over-high dosage can cause problems. Ironically, ginger can occasionally cause digestive upsets in some dogs, and it may be inadvisable to give it where certain health issues are present including if on insulin, receiving anti-inflammatory or heart/blood pressure medication, and should not be given within ten days of surgery as it may have a mild blood-thinning effect. (*See also Herbal Remedies*)

If panting occurs due to worrying, your dog may get very thirsty; bouts of vomiting or diarrhoea can also lead to him becoming dehydrated unless he takes some fluids on board. Fresh water should therefore be made available to him - either provide it in a non-spill travelling bowl or stop frequently to offer him a drink. This second option may be preferable if your dog tends to drink copious amounts due to stress, which can then increase the likelihood of vomiting, as you will be able to control intake, encouraging him to drink little and often. Your dog may not be keen on drinking while in the car, so try offering it while outside. If he doesn't seem interested, offer him a drink again after he has had a chance to stretch his legs and take a break. This may need to be done at a distance from the car, in case the close proximity causes distress.

If he shows a reluctance to drink, you can try encouraging him by introducing a more tempting flavour to the bowl such as chicken broth; it is also possible to buy commercially produced 'drinks' for dogs.

## MEDICATION

Especially in severe cases of motion sickness, medication may be one of the first things you think of reaching out for, after the wet wipes and rolls of kitchen towel. After all, various medications are commonly used with humans who suffer from the same problem, so how bad can they be for dogs?

Drug treatment for travelling issues include those products which will decrease nausea and/or vomiting, and tranquilizers and sedatives to calm dogs which display hyperactive or fearful behaviour in the car. Many of these medications can have worrying side effects, and are not always easy to manage, so we would suggest that you try a holistic approach first, which when combined with sympathetic travel training can often lead to a successful and lasting outcome. If you are really struggling, then do discuss the problems you are having with your vet, who can, if it is felt that drugs may be of benefit, prescribe something which will be both effective and appropriate for your dog. Although some non-prescription medications are available, always arrange for a consultation with your vet before giving them to your dog.

### *Anti-emetic (anti-sickness) drugs*
On the plus side, if these work they can help your dog

to feel a whole lot better – but they can have a downside too. Some cannot be used with very young dogs, and there may be a limit as to how often they can be used; and as they usually need to be given at a specified time - ranging from thirty minutes to up to two hours - before travelling, and because mealtimes may need to be organised around dosing, administration isn't always a simple matter. There may be possible side effects too, such as diarrhoea, vomiting, allergic reactions, dry mouth, drowsiness, and difficulty in urinating.

Always read the accompanying information; and even if it is claimed that such reactions are uncommon occurrences, you should nevertheless be aware of the potential for them, so that you can make an informed decision about their use, and know what indications to keep a watchful eye out for.

Some of the anti-emetic medications commonly used are prescription-only, but others are available off-prescription, and some are human drugs not licensed for veterinary use. Accidental over-dosing can have serious implications; some drugs may also be contraindicated by any health issues your dog has, and/or may interact badly with other medications he may be taking, so we would recommend that you always consult your vet. Do not give your dog any travel-sickness medications you take yourself; even if they can be safely given to children it does not mean they are safe for your dog!

### Tranquillizers and sedatives
Sedatives and tranquillizers may be viewed by some as an option for dogs who are fearful or inclined to be hyperactive or destructive in the car, but should only

be used as an absolute last resort for those animals that must undertake a car journey for some reason, but have difficulty in doing so. Remember that they will do nothing to help address your dog's actual problems, and may not be a suitable option if certain medical conditions are present.

As well as failing to address issues of fear or anxiety, the duration and depth of sedation can often be difficult to predict with any surety, and there is a possibility that your dog may wake sooner than expected, or risk injury stumbling around in a semi-sedated state if the dosage is insufficient.

As sedation usually needs to be given at least half to one hour before you start out, journey timings need to be carefully planned in advance. Dogs are much brighter than they are often given credit for and if yours has seen you packing bags and preparing the car, and worked out that a journey is impending, he may well have already become anxious, and the adrenalin in his system can considerably reduce the effectiveness of the medication.

As with anti-emetics, there may also be possible side-effects; and the other drawback is, of course, that sedation will limit what you can do when you reach your destination, so is really only practical if you need to undertake a long journey, where your dog can rest and recover on arrival.

## 'CALMING' PRODUCTS

Various commercial non-herbal supplements are available which many owners have found to be helpful with nervous dogs. Containing ingredients ranging from casein, a protein found in cow's milk, to B vitamins, magnesium and amino acids such as

Tryptophan, they claim to have a calming effect and to combat the effects of stress.

Most appear to be safe to use, although as always, consult your vet before giving them to your dog, to ensure the product is suitable for him and will not interact adversely with any medication he is taking. Read carefully through all accompanying literature as some products may not be suitable for pregnant or lactating bitches, and most are not intended for long term use. While they will not directly address travelling issues when used solely on their own, they may be helpful when employed on a short term basis to support your dog while working through any anxieties he has.

## MUSIC

Music can have a beneficial calming effect on you as well as your dog, and certainly it will do no harm to try using it in the car. Preferably use recordings rather than the radio, as this gives you more choice and greater control over what you listen to.

Instrumental pieces are best: avoid heavy metal music at all costs as it tends to have an agitating effect, while pop music appears to make little impression either way.

The few studies which have been done seem to indicate that classical music has the most soothing and relaxing influence, although it's best to avoid anything which is too rousing, or has lots of drum rolls or clashing of cymbals going on.

Experiment with different types of music to discover which your dog prefers and has the most profound effect on him, and once you have made your choice, play it half a dozen times or so at home to create familiarity and establish an association of safety and relaxation. Ideally, play it again for half an hour before the journey as well as during it.

If you wish, it is possible to buy 'psychoacoustically designed' music which has been specifically arranged for dogs. *Through a Dog's Ear: Driving Edition* alleges to be even more successful in creating a calming atmosphere than conventional classical recordings, and claims that it has even helped dogs suffering from nausea and motion sickness.

## HOLISTIC OPTIONS

Holistic therapies are becoming increasingly popular for both humans and animals, and in many instances can be very effective – but it should always be remembered that just because a product is labelled as being 'natural' or 'holistic' or is safe for you to use, it doesn't automatically follow that it is either safe or appropriate for your pet.

*Always* follow the manufacturer's instructions, and *always* consult your vet, (or a qualified holistic vet) if your dog has any health problems or is taking any medications before giving him any non-prescription holistic remedies aimed at helping him to cope with travelling. We both feel that wherever possible, it is best to seek expert advice as some holistic modalities require in-depth knowledge and experience in order to achieve the greatest measure of success.

A further argument in favour of seeking expert advice is that although many of these products are generally safe to use and can work well when used in combination with each other, there are exceptions. Essential oils for example, may lessen the effect of homeopathic remedies, and some may not be safe to use where certain health conditions are present, or may be dermal irritants or photoreactive.

## *ACUPRESSURE*

Acupressure is an ancient Eastern healing art which has been used successfully on both humans and animals for at least four thousand years. It can be beneficial in helping to resolve injuries and health issues, can play a part in pain relief, and in generally maintaining good health and vitality.

As well as motion sickness and nausea, it can be useful in reducing the stress levels of dogs who are fearful about travelling.

A core belief of acupressure is that an intangible energetic component called 'chi', which is responsible for life and health, circulates throughout the whole of the body along invisible but very real pathways called meridians.

If a chi energy disruption happens for some reason, it can cause a blockage (or 'stagnation') along the meridian and an imbalance can occur, which can lead to physical and psychological health issues.

Acupuncture and acupressure are both ways of clearing such blockages and enabling the harmonious flow of chi to be restored; this is achieved through stimulation of specific 'acupoints' which are located along the meridians where they run close to the surface of the body.

Acupuncture employs the use of very fine needles which are quickly inserted, while acupressure relies on the use of the hands and fingers instead to apply pressure to the acupoints. Both techniques work very effectively, but only a qualified vet can perform an acupuncture treatment.

Because accurately locating the acupoints does require a certain degree of anatomical knowledge, and there is potential for causing discomfort to your dog if you are incorrect or over-enthusiastic in your technique, we suggest that rather than applying direct pressure you instead simply try gently rubbing or scratching with your fingers, or using light TTouches (see the section on Tellington TTouches) across each of the various acupoint areas shown in the charts. Although this isn't 'proper' acupressure, it can still produce beneficial effects.

If you would like to find out more and learn how to apply a more direct acupressure technique for a deeper effect, we recommend that you attend a course or arrange for some first-hand tuition from a qualified animal acupressure practitioner. Alternatively, you could arrange for a qualified practitioner to give your dog an acupuncture or acupressure treatment.

When working on your dog yourself, please observe the same guidelines as those detailed in the section on Tellington TTouch, and do not enforce contact on your pet if he is concerned about you touching any areas of his body. This may indicate the presence of a health issue and you should ask your vet to investigate further.

We'd suggest only working a few acupoints each time, and only spending 5-15 seconds on each one. Some points may be sore for your dog so work *very* carefully, observing his body language at all times. The area may spasm when you touch it, or your dog may move away or try to nudge your hand away from the area.

If your dog objects to what you are doing, stop and seek the help of a qualified vet or acupressure practitioner. Your intentions may be good but if wrongly applied, may cause discomfort, pain and distress to your dog as well as putting yourself at risk.

Find a warm, quiet and comfortable place for you and your dog, and have the chart of acupoints ready to refer to.

# Bladder Meridian

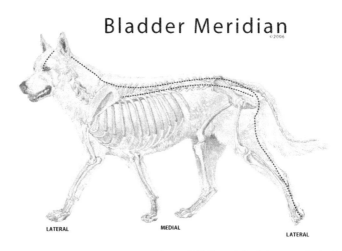

LATERAL                 MEDIAL
                                        LATERAL

*(Diagram © Tallgrass Animal Acupressure Institute)*

Start each session by gently placing one hand on his shoulder. With the other one, following the Bladder Meridian chart above, stroke smoothly and gently along and down his neck and along his body, staying to the side of the spine, then down the hindquarters and along the outside of the hind leg.

It doesn't matter if your dog is sitting, standing or lying down, as long as he is comfortable and feels safe.

Note any areas he may be reluctant for you to touch or which he twitches when you run your hand over. Repeat this procedure three times on each side.

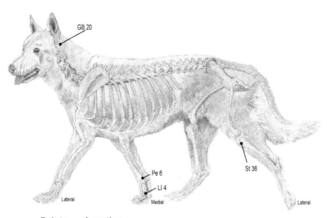

| Points | Location |
|--------|----------|
| LI 4 | Between the dewclaw and 2nd metacarpal bone, at the webbing of the dewclaw. |
| St 36 | Located just lateral to the tibial crest on the lateral aspect of the hindleg. |
| Pe 6 | Located on the inside of the foreleg, about 2 inches above the wrist. |
| GB 20 | At the cranial edge of the wings of the atlas. |

### • Large Intestine 4 (LI 4)

This acupoint is known to tonify and regulate chi so that Stomach chi flows in a downwards direction. LI 4 is beneficial in literally preventing the upchuck response to motion sickness!

### • Stomach 36 (ST 36)

This is considered the Master point for the abdomen and gastro-intestinal tract. This point is used to reduce indigestion and supports the entire digestive process.

### ● Pericardium 6 (Pe 6)

This point is possibly the best known of all the acupoints - many humans find stimulating this point near their wrist very useful in combating motion sickness, and it is the same for dogs.

This point harmonises Stomach chi, thus relieving the sensation of nausea and can prevent vomiting. It can also calm the mind.

### ● Gall Bladder 20 (GB 20)

This point is used to reduce internal upset including anxiety that may induce Stomach chi to go up instead of down. When Stomach chi goes up, it is called "Rebellious Stomach chi," because it is going the wrong way and causing vomiting. GB 20 helps to promote Stomach chi to go in the right direction, down!

### *When to work the points:*

You can work the points daily, and an hour before travelling or doing any travel training.

Start with the highest point, and work from top to bottom, front to back and on both sides of the body.

If someone else is driving and you are able to sit next to your dog during a journey, try working St 36 and Pe 6 points from time to time as you feel necessary – if your dog seems to be fine, then leave him be.

Acupressure should not be used if your dog is pregnant, and consult your vet or a qualified veterinary acupuncturist if your dog is on medication for any health conditions.

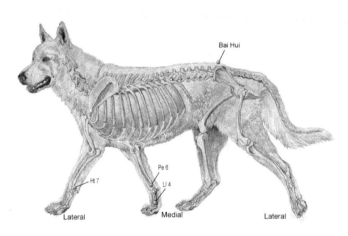

| Points | Location |
|--------|----------|
| LI 4 | At the dewclaw, medial aspect of the foreleg. |
| Ht 7 | Located on the outside of the foreleg, in the deep crease of the carpal joint. |
| Pe 6 | Located on the inside of the foreleg, about 2 inches above the carpal (wrist). |
| Bai Hui | Found on dorsal midline at the lumbosacral space. |

## • Large Intestine 4 (LI 4)

By regulating chi within the body, LI 4 can reduce body tension in general which is helpful in bringing down the dog's stress level.

## • Heart 7 (Ht 7)

This is the go-to acupoint for calming the spirit of the dog. It is a powerful point for clearing fear and anxiety at any time and especially when facing a particularly scary experience.

## ● Pericardium 6 (Pe 6)

Though Pe 6 is known for digestive issues, it also used extensively for calming the mind and relieving anxiety.

## ● Bai Hui

Located on the midline of the sacrum where you can't feel the spinous processes. This point is traditionally called 'Heavens Gate' - most dogs love being scratched there! It generates energy along the spine, and is also a calming point which produces a feeling of wellbeing and is helpful with apprehensive, worried dogs.

## *BACH REMEDIES*

In common with other holistic modalities, Bach Flower Essences (not to be confused with aromatic floral sprays) can be helpful with a wide variety of issues, including travelling.

They are not sedatives or tranquilizers, but act to gently address and rebalance emotions and mental states of mind, which makes them particularly appropriate with dogs who are reactive, fearful, and have unpleasant associations with being in the car.

They can be used in conjunction with conventional as well as homeopathic and herbal remedies and can provide support when working through travel training.

They are very safe to use - as far as we are aware, adverse effects have never been reported; but we would suggest that, as always, you err on the side of safety and check first with your vet before giving them to your pet.

You may find that Bach essences can benefit you as

well as your dog - if you tend to be stressed as a driver, it reduces your driving skills which in turn affects how good a ride your dog gets, while your emotional output can cause him to become anxious or exacerbate any worries he already has.

Bach Flower Essences can be bought over the counter at most high street chemists and health shops as well as online; look for the pet-friendly alcohol-free versions.

Bach Rescue Remedy is probably the best known of all the essences, and can help take the edge off your dog's anxiety if you have to travel, or when working through a travel training programme. Useful in emergency situations or at times of stress, it is a combination of five different flower essences: Star of Bethlehem (shock and trauma), Rock Rose (terror), Clematis (faintness), Impatiens (agitation), and Cherry Plum (loss of control) and is useful for general calming.

You might like to research other flower essences, which will more specifically address your dog's travel issues: choose the remedy or remedies you feel best fit your dog. Don't worry if you choose the 'wrong' one: if it isn't right for your dog it will simply have no effect, and no harm will come of it. Flower essences which may have particular relevance include:

**Vervain:** if there is over-excitable, hyperactive behaviour, particularly in younger dogs where the behaviour is due to youthful over-exuberance.

**Impatiens:** good for reducing stress in highly strung dogs which tend to rush around when anxious, tense or nervous.

**Mimulus:** addresses general fears and anxieties: dogs that whine and tremble: consider Rock Rose for deeper-seated, more extreme fear, or maybe combine Mimulus and Rock Rose together.

**Rock Rose:** where fear borders on terror: panicky behaviour, scrabbling around, destructive behaviour, desperate to escape from the car.

**Cherry plum:** brings calm and helps restore self-control where extreme stress and hysterical, panicky behaviour is present.

**Star of Bethlehem:** helps to release the memory and after-effects of previous trauma.

**Elm:** helps to reduce sensory overload.

**Walnut:** helps in coping with change, new experiences, sights, sounds, and stressful environments so can be useful with young dogs learning to travel in the car.

**Scleranthus:** can be very helpful in cases of nausea due to motion sickness – this is one of the remedies and occasions where flower essences appear to have a direct physical effect as well as on the emotional and psychological mindset.

A single remedy may be sufficient and work very effectively; but where there are several issues, you can combine several essences (up to four) to make up your own mix specifically tailored to your dog. As with homeopathy, the better the match to the individual, the more successful the outcome is likely to be.

You may see very rapid results if the correct remedies have been selected, sometimes within minutes, but it can take longer, so persevere for at least two and preferably three to four weeks. Perversely, the milder the problem is, the longer it can take to see beneficial results; and bear in mind that irregular and missed doses may cause the remedies to be less effective.

### *Administration*

If you want to give multiple remedies it is easiest if you make up a remedy bottle. Take a small clean bottle or jar, fill with around 30 ml of fresh clean water – bottled mineral water for preference – and add to this two drops of each remedy (up to four different flower essences) you have chosen. Put the cap or lid on, shake to mix it and store it in the fridge. Discard anything that is left over after five days and make up a fresh batch.

Give four drops of the remedy you have selected as being most appropriate for your dog, or from your remedy bottle, four times daily; if you are out during the day and can't manage this, then give eight drops twice daily. Don't worry if you accidentally give too many or too few drops – overdosing is virtually impossible, and it is more important that you dose regularly each and every day.

Bach Flower Essences can be administered in various ways. Never try to give them directly into your dog's mouth from the glass dropper just in case he bites it. Instead, put a few drops on your fingers which your dog can lick off, or add them to his drinking water bowl (it will not lose its efficacy when diluted) or to his food, or offer on pieces of dry bread or treats which will absorb the liquid. Bear in mind that if your dog is feeling stressed or nauseous at the time, he may not want to eat, or if he does, may be liable to choke on it. The remedies can also be dropped onto the top of the nose or along the lips where your dog will reflexively lick them off. Alternatively, they can be applied to the pads of the paws, on the belly, or to the acupoint which lies halfway between his ears by dropping the remedy onto the palm of your hand and then stroking it onto the top of his head. If administered externally in this way, dose as frequently as you would if giving them orally. You might also like to try spritzing the remedy into the car interior, either using the Bach Rescue Remedy spray or by putting your choice of remedies into a small re-usable pump-spray bottle. Choose whichever method causes the least stress to your dog, and is easy and safe for you to do.

## *HOMEOPATHY*

Homeopathy addresses the whole body, so can be effective in resolving emotional issues as well as physical problems.

Pioneered and developed by Samuel Hahnemann in the eighteenth century, it is based on the principle that 'like cures like' following his discovery that substances which produced the same symptoms as an ailment, could, when given in much smaller quantities, cure it. These substances are diluted in a special process known as potentisation, and subjected to succussion (vigorous shaking) which increases the homeopathic strength even though the chemical concentration decreases.

Homeopathy is a very safe modality, and if the wrong remedy is chosen, it will simply have no effect and do no harm.

Homeopathic remedies are obtainable from chemists, health shops and online, where they are most commonly supplied as 6c or 30c 'potencies'. This refers to the dilution and succussion of the remedy – the higher the number the more times it has undergone this process and the more powerful the effect may be. Remedies often suggested for travelling issues include:

**Cocculus:** signs of dizziness and nausea, hiccups, spasmodic yawning: symptoms made worse by eating, the smell of food and fresh air: better for lying still. Dogs who benefit from this remedy often have anxious personalities, prone to worrying about their owners. Do not give with Nux vomica or Coffea.

**Argent nit:** used where there is belching, nausea, vomiting, and wind; symptoms are better for cool fresh air, worse for warmth and at night. It is also a likely remedy to use where the dog is generally anxious or fearful about the journey and tends to be restless. Often of benefit with dogs who are jumpy and anxious, but who will challenge their fears, rather than running away from them.

**Petroleum:** where there is nausea, belching and drooling; better in warm air, worse for dampness.

**Tabacum:** motion sickness with severe nausea, vomiting on the least movement; eyes are closed when feeling sick; symptoms are aggravated by tobacco smoke and worse in extremes of hot and cold: better for fresh air and eyes closed: vomiting brings relief.

**Nux vomica:** signs of nausea; vomiting, but with effort, not easily - often retching for some time: better after sleeping, worse after eating. Do not give Nux vomica with Cocculus or Coffea as they are incompatible with each other and will antidote or inactivate.

**Kalium phosphate:** useful for any nervous, anxious, stressed animal, it is especially good for nervous stomachs.

**Ipecac:** where there is much dribbling and drooling of saliva, constant nausea and vomiting; may be worse for lying down.

**Borax:** nausea; the dog shows nervousness and is very sensitive to loud and/or sudden noises: better in cool weather. He may have a great fear of falling and of downward motion – so he may, for example, be happy to jump into the car but reluctant to jump out again.

**Coffea:** signs of restlessness, fidgety, twitchy, on the go and unable to settle, over-excitement before a journey: this type of dog is often a very happy, sensitive and joyous personality; better for warmth and lying down. Do not give with Nux vomica or Cocculus.

**Aconite:** may be helpful where a dog is anxious about travelling or goes into panic mode: very restless and fidgety in the car, finding it hard to settle: better for fresh air and worse for noise and light.

It will do no harm to try any of these remedies; if they are not the right ones for your dog then they will simply have no effect. The success of homeopathy does rely on closely matching the right remedy (or remedies) to the individual, taking into account not only physical symptoms but background, lifestyle, environment, demeanour, character, likes, dislikes, fears, diet, household and family details and responses to various external influences. If the remedies you have chosen are not working, then seek professional help - bear in mind that very often the symptoms can be a manifestation of deeper fears and as such are best dealt with by a homeopathic veterinary practitioner.

Homeopathic remedies come in either liquid, pill or crystal form and need to be stored and administered correctly: the general advice is that they should not be given with food, or close to mealtimes, and should be stored away from strong smells and direct sunlight. Avoid handling them as this can also destroy their efficacy. Keep them in their original container, and if you drop a pill on the floor, discard it.

As they aren't unpleasant tasting there isn't usually a problem with giving them, although you can if necessary crush pills between two spoons into a fold of paper and tip them into your dog's mouth so they stick to his tongue. The liquid remedies can sometimes be easier to manage - you will know your dog and which form will be the simplest to give.

Allow fifteen minutes before or after eating, and at least five minutes between remedies if you are giving more than one. Simply tip into the bottle cap if giving pills or crystals (some bottes have a handy dispenser system that releases single pills into the cap), open your dog's mouth, and tip in. With liquids, place a few drops on to your dog's tongue or lips. Do not let the cap come into contact with your dog's mouth. If you do find any difficulties in dosing, try adding ten drops of a liquid remedy to his water bowl - but remember just how acute a dog's senses are, and check that he continues to happily drink from that bowl.

Give the 30c potency of the remedy you think is most appropriate for your dog one hour before your journey, again on departure and then every one to three hours during the journey - but only if necessary. Results from homeopathy can sometimes be surprisingly quick!

## APPLIED ZOOPHARMACOGNOSY

Essential oils and floral sprays (plant essences in a more diluted form, and also called aromatic waters – not to be confused with Bach and other flower essences), can be another powerful and effective way of helping your dog if he suffers from motion sickness or finds car travel stressful or frightening.

Applied Zoopharmacognosy is not quite the same as aromatherapy, which you may be familiar with in a human context: an AZ practitioner is more akin to a herbalist who possesses an in-depth knowledge of pharmacokinetics than an Aromatherapist. The essential oils are used differently with animals, employing a process of 'self-selection' whereby the most suitable oil or oils are selected by allowing your dog to do the actual choosing himself. This is done by offering him in turn those which you think are likely to be the most helpful. This is done slowly, with the open bottle held approximately 30 cm to one metre away from his nose, and his reaction to each carefully observed. It is crucial that only high quality oils, prepared especially for this purpose are used - those intended for use in burners are not suitable.

Oils should never be enforced on your dog with burners and diffusers, or applied to his body, unless he clearly indicates that he wants this. If you wish to use a burner or diffuser in your home for your own benefit, then do leave a door open so that your dog can move to another room if he wishes.

## *Offering oils*

Before offering any oils to your dog, you should take the time to create a good working environment. In a multi-pet household, other animals should be shut away while working with the oils; but your dog should have the option available at all times of leaving the room you are both in. Prop the door open and leave him off the leash so he is always free to move away if he wishes. It is also nice to have a comfortable dog bed in the room so that if he wants to, he can lie down while working with the oils; and ensure that a bowl of drinking water is available. Oils should be offered at a time when your dog has few distractions; not, for example, near to the time when he is usually fed or when he is anticipating going for a walk. Plenty of time should be set aside, as some dogs may want to work with oils for an extended period, especially the first time they are offered. Different dogs may choose different oils for a similar issue; some may choose more than one, and they may also need the oils to be offered in a specific order, so finding the right oils can be a very individual matter. Upon being offered the oils, your dog's responses need to be carefully noted and correctly interpreted.

The process of narrowing down and then fine-tuning the most appropriate oil or oils is not always a simple procedure. Knowledge of the actions of the oils is essential: they can be *very* potent, and some may not be appropriate to use where certain health conditions are present or if your dog is pregnant or receiving any medication. They may also lessen or extinguish completely the effect of any homeopathic remedies that are being given.

If you wish to explore this fascinating modality, we suggest that you first read Caroline Ingraham's informative book *Help Your Dog Heal Itself,* which explains the whole process in more detail than there is room for here, together with details of a number of oils. Alternatively, you could arrange a consultation with an AZ practitioner, who will have a wide range of oils which your dog can select from. Do check that the practitioner is up-to-date in their knowledge; a register is currently being compiled – see the Contacts and Resources section for further details.

One final note: what your dog needs may not be what *you* need. You may have adverse reactions to certain oils, such as disliking the smell, or finding that it makes you feel sleepy or unwell. On a car journey this could obviously prove hazardous!

## *PET REMEDY*

A product called Pet Remedy has recently become widely available in pet shops and online, bought as either a spray, diffuser or battery operated atomiser, and many owners have reported good effects in a variety of stressful situations. The manufacturer's information states that it is a low dosage Valerian blend (it also contains Vetiver, Sweet Basil and Sage) but because it is based on essential oils, we would suggest that you observe the same general guidelines as for Applied Zoopharmacognosy: first see if your dog likes the smell while in the house, by offering him the option of sniffing at the spray applied to your hand or a tissue, or if using the diffuser, leaving a door open so that he can either stay or leave the room if he wishes.

## HERBAL REMEDIES

Herbalism is one of the most ancient forms of medicine and you may well find a few traditional and inexpensive remedies in your kitchen cupboard in the form of herbal teabags. Chamomile, spearmint, peppermint and ginger can all be good pick-me-ups after travelling, helping to calm the nerves and settle the stomach. An infusion can be made using a teabag, allowed to cool and then offered to your dog to sniff at and to drink if he wishes. Do not, however, force feed it to him if he shows no interest in it, and ensure that clean fresh drinking water is available too.

Nowadays you will find plenty of commercial herbal preparations available online and stocked in pet stores, which aim to relieve travel sickness or reduce general anxiety. Herbal remedies should however, always be treated with great respect and used with care; we suggest that for your pet's welfare you always err on the side of caution and consult a vet knowledgeable in the use of herbs. Always bear in mind that just because a product is advertised as being 'natural' or 'traditional' it doesn't mean that it is either safe or suitable for your dog. Some may be harmful to use where certain health issues are present, and they should never be given alongside conventional drugs except under the advice of a veterinary surgeon with appropriate knowledge and experience in this area, in case they conflict with the medication or even combine with it to produce toxic doses. Care should also be exercised in using herbal preparations in conjunction with homeopathy or Applied Zoopharmacognosy.

Do not give your dog herbal preparations formulated for humans except under veterinary advice, as what is good for people isn't always good for dogs. Even where a product is labelled as being specifically for dogs, do still check and research all the ingredients and once again, consult with a vet if you have any concerns. Many of the 'calming' herbal remedies contain ingredients including skullcap, valerian, passionflower, marshmallow, chamomile, lemon balm, vervain, and lime flowers, all of which are commonly considered as being relatively safe in small doses – but we have spotted some which also contain hops, the flower cones of which are generally regarded as being toxic to dogs. Even those herbs deemed to be 'relatively safe' are not necessarily appropriate for all dogs: valerian for example, may be unsuitable for dogs who are pregnant or suffering from liver disease, and shouldn't be given prior to surgical procedures requiring anaesthesia. Dosage guidelines should be very carefully followed – more is not better, and can often be harmful if given in excess; there may also be cumulative effects with some herbs, making them unsuitable for long term use.

Although an appropriate, carefully selected herbal remedy may help in taking the edge off fears and reducing stress levels if your dog is an anxious passenger in the car, it is unlikely that used on its own, it will prove to be a miracle cure for your dog's travelling issues. It may however be beneficial when used to provide support during training programmes – although do observe your dog carefully, as with some individuals the opposite of the desired effect can occur, and he may become more hyperactive or anxious.

## TELLINGTON TTOUCH METHOD®

Devised nearly forty years ago by Linda Tellington Jones, and developed in conjunction with her sister Robyn Hood, Tellington TTouch is often confused with massage. It is actually very different, and as well as the special 'TTouches' employs a varied system of exercises which include groundwork and body wraps.

The Tellington TTouch Method - or TTouch® (pronounced Tee Touch) for short – has a proven track record for helping animals with a wide range of issues, including motion sickness and other travel-related issues. It is a kind, non-invasive, generally well accepted and empathic way of working with animals which is easy to learn, simple and safe to apply, and can have profound effects on the lives of animals and on the people who care for them.

The Tellington TTouch Method is based on the principle that posture and behaviour are inextricably linked, with posture affecting behaviour and vice versa. By improving posture, balance and movement, beneficial physical, psychological and emotional changes are produced, with self-confidence and self-control increasing. Mind and body begin to work together in harmony and unwanted behaviours diminish or disappear entirely. This is not some far-fetched or whimsical theory, but one which has been successfully demonstrated time and time again, both with Tellington TTouch and in other modalities which focus on posture, such as Alexander Technique.

TTouch provides you with the tools to make changes for the better to your dog's posture – and because poor balance is frequently an underlying cause of travelling issues such as motion sickness and an inability to settle, it can be very successful in remedying them.

### *'Reading' your dog*

It is often forgotten just how closely connected posture and behaviour are, even though we constantly use phrases such as having cold feet, gritting our teeth, or tearing our hair out to describe states of mind. We can also perceive how someone is feeling by observing their posture: a happy person will literally be 'standing tall', walking with a bounce in their step, head up and quite possibly a smile on their face. Conversely a depressed person will appear to be drooping, hunched up, with rounded shoulders and a slower, dragging stride.

Just as body language can reflect a state of mind, so the reverse can be true, with poor posture or the presence of 'tension patterns' directly influencing the mental and emotional processes and dictating behaviour.

Dogs with physical and/or behavioural issues frequently exhibit tension patterns. These can develop for a variety of reasons, including physical injury, health issues, frightening experiences and emotional trauma. The tension produced and sustained in specific areas of the body promotes different responses; for example, a dog which holds tension through his hind quarters will often tend to be fearful – these individuals also often suffer from travelling issues.

Tension patterns show up in many ways. There may be a very hot or cold area on the body: the skin may feel stiff and immobile rather than sliding freely across the underlying tissues: changes in coat colour or texture may be seen, or greasy or dry scurfy patches: swirls and changes of direction in the way the hairs grow may be noticed. Muscling and wear and tear on the nails and pads may differ from one side to the other … It is a fascinating study, and as you learn to look at your dog in more detail, you will learn a lot about him which can make it easier to help him. More detailed information on tension patterns and how to identify them can be found in Sarah Fisher's book *Unlock Your Dog's Potential*.

Observing your dog is an important part of TTouch work, but it will also benefit you in all other areas of your relationship; noting your dog's posture, how he moves and responds to his environment and the situations he finds himself in will tell you a lot about how he is feeling physically and provide an invaluable key to his mental processes and emotional state.

Learning to 'read' your dog's posture will help you to decide which TTouches to use and where to use them: when to start, and when to stop: and help ensure that you stay safe. You may need to exercise care when handling or performing TTouches on areas which hold a lot of tension as your dog may be reluctant for you to touch him there, and it may even cause him discomfort when you do. Always keep this latter point in mind, and do read carefully through the section on safety.

## *Tellington TTouch Body Work: The TTouches*

The special 'TTouches' involve gently moving the skin in various ways. They are the foundation of the Tellington TTouch Method and provide a positive way of calming and reassuring, helping your dog to relax, releasing tension and lowering his stress levels. Anyone can do them, no specialised knowledge of anatomy is needed, and they can be used either on their own, in conjunction with other modalities or with Tellington TTouch equipment such as body wraps (explained further on). You can learn how to do the TTouches by reading a book, watching a video, attending a workshop or demo or asking a practitioner to visit (details can be found in the Contacts & Resources section), and once the basic skills are learnt you can apply them anywhere, anytime, whenever your pet has need of them. It takes only a short time to learn how to produce a beneficial effect, although the more you practise, the better you will become at it.

The TTouches will help to prepare your dog for car journeys by developing his self-confidence, self-control and balance. Introduce them at home first so they are familiar, pleasurable and reassuring to your dog, and you are at ease about doing them. During car training try and do some TTouches with your dog every day so that it is a normal part of your routine. Once both of you are confident and calm, you can begin doing very short TTouch bodywork sessions near to, and then in the car - first while it is stationary and with the door open, then with the engine running, and working up to shutting the door and having someone moving the car forward a few metres at a time. More details about travel training and using TTouches during it will be found later in this book.

### How to introduce TTouch Bodywork

While doing the TTouches be sure to not lean over your dog, as this might intimidate or frighten him. It is safer for you and more comfortable for your dog if you position yourself to the side of, and just behind his head, so that you are both facing in the same direction. This will enable you to see him and to monitor his responses clearly but without staring directly at him which he may find confrontational. It also makes it easy for him to move away if he wishes, without having to go through you in order to do so.

Bear in mind that if your dog's stress affects you – which it may do even if you aren't directly aware of it – it can be easy to start doing the TTouches rather fast. This can then have the opposite effect to the one you are trying to produce: generally, doing the TTouches slowly is calming while going faster tends to be stimulating. Be sensitive to indications from your dog that he has had enough and needs a break. You will find that lots of short sessions often work better than one long one, and can easily be fitted into odd moments during the day when you have a few minutes to spare. We suggest that the longest you work with your dog should be no more than around twenty minutes, and incorporating a few mini-breaks into the session if needed. Signs that your dog may need a break include him looking unsettled, moving away from you, becoming distracted, and fidgeting. Stop for a while and allow your dog to reposition himself. If he readily settles down for some more work, continue, but if he responds again in a similar way, then it is probably time to end the session and try again another time. Very often you will find that you see further improvement after you have finished a session – and what may have been difficult for your dog to cope with today, may be easier for him tomorrow. Give him the benefit of the doubt, keep sessions short and listen to your dog.

## *Before you start!*

Before you get started on using the TTouches, for maximum benefit and to avoid inadvertently stressing your dog or compromising your safety, remember the following golden rules:

▶ **If your dog wishes to move away** while doing the TTouches, allow him to do so.

▶ **Let him choose his position:** do not insist that he stands if he feels more comfortable sitting or lying down.

▶ **Practice doing each of the TTouches on your own arms** or on a partner or friend's arms or back before trying them on your pet. This will help you to appreciate just how light and subtle you can be. Another human can also give you feedback on how it feels and help you to improve.

▶ **Concentrating on what you are doing** can sometimes make you stiff and tense, which will make the TTouches feel unpleasant to the recipient. Try to relax and keep your breathing deep and regular. Allowing your dog to hear you breathe deeply and *slowly* will also encourage him to match his rate of breathing to yours, aiding calmness.

► **Just the weight of your hand is enough to move the skin** while performing each of the TTouches, and you can make the contact even lighter still if your dog appears wary of the work. At no time should you press into the body; you are only working with the skin.

► **Make each of your TTouches as slow as possible.**

► **Constantly observe your dog's body language,** as this can indicate his state of mind. You will find Sarah Fisher's book *Unlock Your Dog's Potential* and Turid Rugaas' book *On Talking Terms with Dogs* helpful; but unless you have a lot of experience in this area it can be easy to misinterpret responses or miss more subtle ones. You may therefore find it helpful initially to arrange a session with a Tellington TTouch practitioner who can help you develop your powers of observation.

► **TTouch is something** we do *with* our animals not *to* them. Break it down into smaller steps if needed, or start the work in the Confidence Course (you will find more details about this in the following pages).

Better still, contact a guild certified Tellington TTouch Practitioner for help if you are having any difficulties in applying the work.

► **Should your dog show concern** about you touching certain parts of his body, return to a place where he is less anxious, and when he relaxes try gradually approaching the difficult area again. If there are other signs such as stiffness, or tautness or changes in temperature of the skin, or changes in the hair colour, direction and texture of the coat, it may indicate the presence of a physical problem; ask your vet to investigate further.

### *Staying safe*

You can do TTouches all over your dog's body, but **observe him closely** as you do so. We cannot emphasise too often that the most affectionate and placid of dogs can behave unpredictably when stressed and may strike out unexpectedly if he is frightened or feels unwell. If you lack experience in reading canine body language, a Tellington TTouch practitioner will be able to help you in developing this essential skill.

As has already been explained, fear, arousal and physical conditions are usually evident in your dog's posture as tension patterns. When you gently touch those areas the skin may feel taut and the muscles hard and tight. You may even see changes in the coat texture, and the tail might be clamped down tightly between the hind legs. If you can release the tension in these places it can make a big difference, with a more relaxed posture producing a correspondingly calmer and more relaxed state of mind: but using the TTouches to help achieve this needs to be managed with great tact and subtlety as your dog may be particularly sensitive to contact in these areas at first.

Be very gentle and watch him carefully at all times, adapting your actions according to whether they indicate a decreasing or increasing level of concern. You will find reading Turid Rugaas' book *On Talking Terms With Dogs*, and Sarah Fisher's book *Unlock Your Dog's Potential* which contains detailed information on tension patterns, invaluable guides in helping to develop your observational skills and in interpreting what you see. If he shows a low level of concern, try using a sheepskin mitten, balled-up sock or sponge to do the TTouches with. Remember to be very gentle: and in any places where a lot of tension is present making the skin and muscles very tight, it is especially essential to be light, slow and soft in your movements, so you don't cause discomfort. Doing just one or two TTouches and then pausing can also help the work to be more acceptable.

The TTouches can cause many different sensations through the body which at first may feel a little weird to your dog. Bear in mind that just because he is tolerating something, it doesn't necessarily mean that he is enjoying it, so act with caution and keep observing his responses closely – although not by staring hard at him which he may find alarming!

If he is still concerned or the level of anxiety increases, don't enforce the TTouches. Work instead on a different area which your dog finds easy to cope with; the shoulder perhaps. As he begins to relax a little you may be able to gradually begin to approach and work on the challenging area, very briefly at first, slowly building it up one TTouch at a time.

If you are at all unsure, don't persist but seek help from an experienced practitioner. If your dog has an old injury be particularly careful when approaching the site of it. Even though it may have occurred a long time ago and be completely healed now, he may still be defensive about that part of his body and show anxiety about you touching it, especially when he is stressed. In some cases there may still be residual discomfort in the area even though to all outward appearances he seems to be fully recovered. He may also have a fear of the memory of pain in that area. If there is any doubt in the matter, ask your vet to check it out.

**Remember!**
**If your dog doesn't like what you're doing, try:**
using a lighter pressure:
*and/or*
a faster or slower speed:
*and/or*
using a soft-bristled paint brush, sheepskin mitten or balled-up sock to introduce the work
*and/or*
working on a different part of the body:
*and/or*
a different TTouch
*and/or*
stopping for a short period and letting your dog move around and think about the experience before trying again
*and/or*
making sessions shorter - some dogs can only cope with a few minutes or a few TTouches at a time to begin with. Be patient, increasing the number of TTouches and length of each session slowly
*and/or*
starting with TTouch ground work and seeking the help of an experienced Tellington TTouch practitioner

## The Tellington TTouches

There are many different TTouches, many named after the animals that inspired them. We have included a few simple and effective ones here that you might like to try and which can be especially helpful with travelling issues. Once you are familiar with them you may like to add others to your repertoire. You can find out more by reading the books recommended in the Contacts and Resources section at the end of this book or by attending a workshop or demonstration, or working one-to-one with a TTouch practitioner. You can also see the TTouches being demonstrated online by visiting You Tube and searching for Tellington TTouch for dogs - you will find plenty of video clips.

If you are a little unsure about reading your dog's body language and want to check that he is comfortable with the body work, simply do one or two repetitions of the TTouch you are performing and stop. Take your hands off your dog and move back a little from him.

If he re-engages with you by looking in your direction, moving closer, nudging your arm or vocalising by maybe softly whining, whilst looking and moving towards you, then continue doing a few more TTouches. Check in often with him, by regularly stopping and asking for permission to continue. If however your dog moves away when you stop, let him. He may need a drink, or to 'think' about how the work feels. Often he will return and re-engage with you and you can continue but if not, don't force it. Go and do something else instead - play a game, go for a toilet break or finish the session there. Some dogs really do need the work drip fed in micro sessions so be led by your dog and give him the choice.

## *LLAMA TTOUCH*

Llama TTouches are very soothing and calming, so are useful for dogs which are timid, nervous, or anxious about being touched on certain parts of the body. The Llama TTouch can also be a great way to introduce the circular TTouches such as the Clouded Leopard, as it feels less intense.

**1.**

Use the back of your fingers, or the back of your hand. Gently and slowly stroke along your dog's body going with the direction of the coat, and keeping your fingers slightly curved so they are nice and soft, rather than stiff. Do this two or three times, then stop and watch your dog's response – whether he moves away or leans towards you, seeking more contact.

*(photo: Toni Shelbourne)*

If he is comfortable with the contact, widen the area to include all of him including down the legs and along the jaw line. As well as feeling cooler, using the back of your hand to do TTouches may be less threatening and more readily accepted by some dogs. If you note any anxiety stay only briefly in that area before returning to a point (such as the shoulder) where he is more comfortable.

## 2.

As your dog begins to relax and grow more confident about you making physical contact, in addition to stroking with the back of your fingers or hand, try making circular movements as well as stroking ones. Very lightly and gently move the skin as you make each circle, rather than sliding over the coat.

Try visualising a clock face on your dog's body 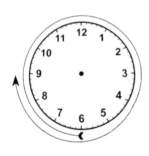 beneath your hand or fingers: your aim is to move the skin, going in a clockwise direction, from the point where the six is, all the way around the clock face and back to six again. When you reach six continue without pausing around to the nine so that you have completed one full circle plus a quarter of another one. Pause and then move to another part of the body. Ensure the skin feels as though you are lightly lifting not dragging it as you start each circle - experiment on your own arm to check.

Make each circle as slow as possible, staying soft and light and noting any signs of concern from your dog; if you do spot any, simply stop for a few moments and/or return to a place on his body where he is more accepting of this body work.

## *ZEBRA TTOUCH*

This is a good TTouch to use with dogs who are overly sensitive about contact, and who may dislike being petted. It's also great for gaining the attention of a nervous and excitable dog, and for calming an anxious one.

**1.**

Position yourself to one side of your dog – he can be sitting, standing or lying down. Start with your fingers and thumb relaxed and gently curved. Resting the hand on the top of his shoulder, slide it downwards, allowing your thumb and fingers to spread apart as it moves downwards, towards the floor or the feet of your dog.

**2.**

As your hand comes back up towards the spine, allow the fingers to loosely close together again. Keep the pressure light, but firm enough that you don't tickle.

*(photo: Sarah Fisher)*

**3.**

Change the angle of your hand slightly each time you complete an upwards or downwards movement so that your hand travels along the length of your dog's body from shoulder to hindquarters in a zigzag pattern.

When you've finished, switch sides and repeat, unless he is lying flat on his side rather than on his chest, in which case just work on the area you can reach.

## CLOUDED LEOPARD & RACCOON TTOUCHES

Because this circular TTouch helps to build trust and improve co-ordination and the ability to learn, it can be really helpful with dogs which are fearful, nervous, stressed and insecure. The Clouded Leopard TTouch can be used all over the body, even in areas such as the tail and face. Generally it is easiest to start on your dog's shoulder area and work out from there, returning to this area if need be.

**1.**

Position yourself to the side and slightly behind your dog. Rest one hand lightly on his body. Softly curve the fingers of your other hand, so that it looks a bit like a leopard's paw. Lightly place the pads of the fingers on your dog's body, with the thumb a little apart from them to help steady your hand. Your wrist should be straight and relaxed at all times to enable the fingers and wrist to rotate as you perform the movement.

**2.**

Using the pads of the finger tips, gently move your dog's skin in a clockwise circle about 1 cm in diameter. Maintain the same speed for the whole movement. It helps if you imagine that your fingers are travelling around a clock face: start each circle where the six would be and move in a clockwise direction all the way around the dial – but when you return to the six position again, keep on going to nine o'clock on the clock face so that you have completed one full circle plus a quarter of another one. Try to make your circles as slow as possible.

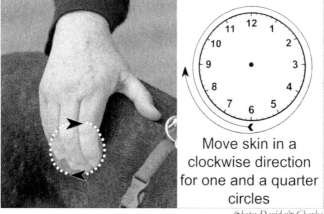

Move skin in a clockwise direction for one and a quarter circles

*(photo: David & Charles)*

**3.**

Keep your wrist and fingers relaxed, and maintain a light but consistent pressure and speed. Do not press into your dog's skin – use no more than just the weight of your hand. After completing each TTouch, stop, and keeping your hand in contact with your dog, pause for a slow breath and then slide your fingers lightly across the coat to a new spot about a hands' width away and begin another circle.

**4.**

Remember to start each circle at the 'six' point, with six being the point nearest to the ground. Ensure that the skin feels as though you are lightly lifting not dragging it as you start each circle - experiment on your own arm to check.

**5.**

Remember that you should be moving the skin with your fingers, rather than allowing your fingers to glide over the surface. If your dog is long coated, you may find it more effective to lightly reposition your fingers into the coat slightly so you can more easily feel his skin.

**6.**

When working over bony areas, or places where he is concerned about being touched, make your contact with your dog's body much lighter, so you are hardly touching him at all while still moving the skin under your fingers. If the skin feels tight, do not try and force it to move, but try making the circles using a larger surface area (by using either the whole of your hand or half the length of your fingers) and continue to use the lightest of pressures and to be very slow in your movement.

**7.**

If your dog doesn't like 'connected' TTouches (ie when you link each TTouch by sliding your fingers across the skin from the circle you have just completed to the place where you are going to start the next one, maintaining a constant light contact) try lifting your hand after each circle instead and gently placing it somewhere else on his body.

Experiment to see which works best for your dog, and bear in mind that preferences may change from day to day or even hour to hour. Sometimes working randomly over your dog's body can grab the attention of the nervous system better than 'connected' TTouches.

**8.**

If your dog still appears reluctant about allowing you to work on certain areas, move back to a place where he enjoys the feel of the TTouch and dip in and out of the areas of concern as described previously. For some dogs, the Clouded Leopard may feel quite intense: if it is too much for him initially try the Llama or Zebra TTouch instead.

**9.**

Try changing your hand position slightly to develop into the **_Raccoon TTouch_** – this is a similar circular movement as the Clouded Leopard but performed using the very tips of the fingers rather than the pads.

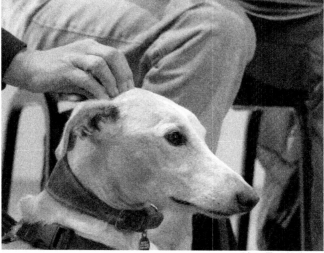

*(photo: Toni Shelbourne)*

This makes the movement smaller and more intense. It can be used all over the body and is especially useful when working around small, more sensitive areas such as around the base of the ears, on the paws and between the toes.

Tiny circular Raccoon TTouches done close together on the legs and paws will help improve balance, and give your dog greater awareness of his feet and the surfaces he stands on.

Start this TTouch at the top of each leg with each circle progressing further down towards the feet. Slide your fingers across the skin between each one for added awareness.

**10.**

If your dog fidgets, either return to the top of the leg and start again or try a different TTouch on another area of the body for a short time before coming back to the legs.

Alternatively try introducing touch to your dog's leg using a soft artists' paint brush, a sheepskin mitten, sponge or even balled-up socks. These items can feel more neutral and will sometimes be more acceptable to your dog than a human hand. Using a brush also enables you to maintain a little distance from your dog, which may help him to tolerate the interaction. Stroke the leg first using the length, not the tip, of the brush hairs, and once he is relaxed about this, perform some of the circular TTouches, again with the side of the bristles. Later you will be able to use your hand on his leg, but it may take several short sessions spread over a number of days to achieve this. Don't try to rush the process!

**11.**

As the legs are bony, make your contact as light as

possible, so you are hardly touching your dog at all while still gently moving the skin under your fingers. Work towards being able to perform Raccoon TTouches down his legs and all over the feet including the toes, paws, pads and between these areas.

Working all over the muzzle too will help his jaw relax and aid with issues such as barking and vocalizing while in the car.

## *EAR WORK*

Ear work can have a wonderfully calming, comforting and soothing effect, helping to lower stress levels and heart rate when done slowly. The majority of dogs enjoy Ear work, and most owners naturally stroke their dog's ears anyway. Ear work is easy to perform before and whilst travelling and is an excellent TTouch for motion sickness sufferers. Queasy feelings can sometimes persist for a while after the car has stopped, so doing more Ear work at the end of your journey will aid in settling his stomach.

**1.**

Position yourself so that both you and your dog are facing in the same direction. Lightly place one hand on his body. Use the back of your other hand to stroke softly along the outside of one ear.

**2.**

If your dog is happy about this, cup your hand around the ear and stroke from the base to the tip. Try to mould as much of your hand as possible around his ear for maximum contact. If your dog has upright ears work in an upwards direction: if they flop downwards, work in a horizontal outwards and downwards direction.

**3.**

Next, take the ear between the thumb and curved forefingers of one hand so that you only have one layer of ear flap between fingers and thumb. Slide them along the length of the ear, working from the base right out to the end or tip. Move your hand slightly each time you begin a new stroke so that you cover every part of the ear. Be gentle and work slowly to help calm and relax.

*(photo: David & Charles)*

At the tip of the ear is an acupressure 'shock' point: make a small circle there with the tip of your forefinger to stimulate it, and then slide your fingers off. This is beneficial for dogs that are habitually nervous.

**4.**

If your dog is holding his ears in a furled, pinned or high ear carriage, very gently unfurl them as you slide along each ear, bringing it into a more natural, relaxed position. Posture can directly affect behaviour, so if the ears are relaxed the rest of the body will tend to follow suit.

## 5.

The ears of some dogs may have a rather taut connection to the head and can feel very stiff and tight – especially when they are feeling stressed or aroused.

In such instances, try a few small circular Raccoon TTouches (see the section on the Clouded Leopard and Raccoon TTouches above) around the base or gently move the whole of your dog's ear in a circular motion to help release the tension. The emphasis *must* be on small and subtle movements – while you want to try and relax the ear and surrounding tense area, if you are forcible you may inadvertently cause discomfort.

In Traditional Chinese Medicine, the Triple Heater Meridian which governs digestion as well as respiration and reproduction runs around the base of the ears (see also the section on acupressure) so doing gentle Raccoon TTouches there can also be benefical for dogs suffering from nausea.

## 7.

If your dog appears to dislike ear work and has floppy ears, try moulding your hand over one and gently holding it against his head. Very slowly and gently move your whole hand in a circular movement, so that his head supports his ear.

Make the circle small so that it is a subtle movement; he may prefer it being circled in an anticlockwise direction to a clockwise one.

If he still finds this challenging try wearing a sheepskin mitten or glove to diffuse the sensation even further. You may find that this will help to reduce any concerns he has and to become more tolerant about Ear work.

If he continues to show concern, do ask your vet to check his ears, mouth and neck, as there may be an underlying physical reason for his unease.

## *TAIL WORK*

The tail is integral to balance, so if it is inflexible it can influence your dog's ability to cope in a moving car.

Dogs who are frightened will instinctively stiffen and tuck their tails, but those who lack good physical poise or are elderly will also often exhibit tension in this area. Helping to release both physical and emotional tension held in the tail can therefore be key to assisting him to cope with travelling.

Although Tail Work can help to increase confidence and balance, do not however, assume that your dog will be happy for you to handle his tail or touch him around his hindquarters. Many dogs who suffer from motion sickness and other travelling issues will find Tail Work very challenging; those who hold a lot of tension in these areas may find it difficult to tolerate contact there and may react defensively, so introduce it over a number of sessions, dipping in and out, and interspersing it with other TTouches.

If in doubt, start to introduce touch to the tail with the Llama or the Clouded Leopard TTouches. You can do this while your dog is sitting so that the floor supports his tail.

If he has long hair, you can also try very gently sliding small sections of hair between your fingers from the root to the tip. Do not pull at the hair, but do not be so light that you produce a tickly sensation, and keep your movements slow and smooth.

This TTouch may be too difficult for your dog to cope with in the car itself but ensure you have done plenty prior to travelling, so that the tail feels loose and flexible.

**1.**

While your dog is standing or lying down, with one hand gently take hold of the tail at its base, near his bottom.

Lightly support it from underneath with your fingers, and with your thumb lying on top, the tip of it facing towards your dog's head. Lightly place your other hand on your dog's hindquarters or under the thigh.

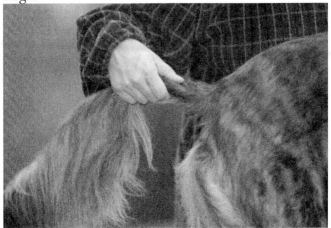

*(photo: David & Charles)*

## 2.

Move the tail slowly and gently in both clockwise and then anti-clockwise directions, making sure that you keep within a comfortable range of movement.

These movements need to be tiny and it can be very easy to over-exaggerate them, so it is a good idea to practise on your own fingers first to see just how little movement is needed to create an effect, and then to apply the same gentle and subtle rotation to your dog's tail.

At first the tail may feel rather wooden and hard to move; work on it for very short periods if your dog shows reluctance for you to touch him in this area, and be very tactful and gentle.

After a while you should notice that the range of movement gradually increases and that your dog becomes happier to have you perform this TTouch. This can take time and several sessions for some dogs.

**3.**

If your dog is very nervous, or clamps his tail down, don't try and pull it out but instead cup the palm of your hand over the top of his tail where it joins his body and gently make small clockwise and anticlockwise circular movements.

From this you can progress to gently holding your dog's tail against one of his own hind legs and then, starting from the base, using the whole of your hand to do circular TTouches along its length all the way down to the tip.

Complete each circle with a pause before sliding a little further down the tail and repeating. Fit in as many circles as you can.

*(photo: David & Charles)*

**4.**

As well as circling the tail, you can also perform a 'pearling' action along the whole length of the tail: slide your hand along the tail, from base to tip, with your fingers in the same position as in step 1.

Each time you feel a vertebra, gently rock it in a downward and inwards movement towards the dog's body. This must be done very, very gently, without exaggerating the movement and while paying very close attention to your dog's responses. Again, you can practise this on your own finger before trying it on your dog.

**5.**

No tail? No problem – even if your dog's tail is docked, you can still gently work the stump using the circular rotations or by doing Raccoon TTouches along its length.

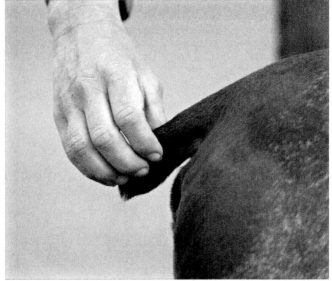

*(photo: David & Charles)*

## *PYTHON LIFT TTOUCH*

Python Lifts can help to release tension in the neck, shoulders, back and legs. This makes it a very beneficial TTouch to assist in improving the balance of dogs who struggle to find stability in the car (which may then trigger motion sickness) and can also help to reduce excitability.

## 1.

Place one hand on your dog's chest to lightly support and maintain a connection with him – allow him to move forward or away if he wishes. Gently place the other hand, palm down, on top of your dog's neck. Keep your wrist and fingers relaxed so they follow his body's contours.

*(photo: Toni Shelbourne)*

Slowly breathe out, and as you do so, use just enough

pressure with your hand to very gently and slowly move the skin up towards the back of his head. Use only the very lightest amount of pressure – the weight of your hand, or less, will be quite sufficient.

Take care not to press down or to squeeze with your fingers. Don't try to move the skin too far as this will be uncomfortable – rather than going to the full limit of its stretch, go only about half the way or less.

**2.**

Maintaining this 'lift' of the skin, pause for a count of three, still breathing out. Then, as you breathe in again, very slowly slide the skin back to its starting point. Aim to maintain the same constant and consistent level of contact the whole time, and try to take twice as long to guide the skin down as it took to carry it upwards; so if it took two seconds to slide it upwards, take four seconds to move it back down.

**3.**

Pause again for a second or two, then lighten the contact of your hand slightly, so you can glide it a little further along the neck, and repeat. If your dog is happy about it, continue on along the neck towards the withers, and then along the length of his back.

**4.**

Next, try Python Lifts on the legs. Move around your dog to work on each leg, rather than moving him, and avoid leaning over his body, which may cause him concern and may lead to lack of subtlety and co-ordination in your movements. If your dog is elderly or has physical issues that make standing difficult for him while you do this TTouch, you can still perform it while he is lying on his side. When working on the front legs, mould the whole of your hand around the top of the foreleg, keeping your hand and wrist relaxed and flexible. On the back legs, begin by moulding both hands around the upper thigh, with the thumbs parallel with your index fingers.

**5.**

Starting at the top of each leg, on a slow exhalation of your breath, gently move the skin in an upwards direction towards the body. As before, use only the very lightest of pressure with your hands, and do not squeeze or grip the limb. As when doing Python Lifts along the neck and back, do not take the skin to its full stretch, but pause about half the way or less. Maintain the upwards lift of the skin, still breathing out.

**6.**

As you breathe in again, slowly return the skin to its starting point. Keep the same level of contact throughout the upwards and downwards movement and the pause, and try to take twice as long on the way down than on the upward movement.

**7.**

Glide your hand a short way down to another section of leg and repeat. Do not do this TTouch directly over the joints, but otherwise, continue in this way until you reach the foot. How many Python Lifts you do will depend on how far you move your hand each time and the length of your dog's legs – aim for at least four or five. Make sure they are not too far apart or it can produce a disconnected sensation.

Remember always to breathe out as you 'lift' and in as you slowly release.

**8.**

Finish by stroking your cupped hand down the whole of the leg from the top down to the foot; pause as you reach it and then slide your fingers off the ends of the toes and onto the floor.

This will help to give him greater awareness of the floor beneath his feet and will aid in helping him to balance more proficiently in the car. If your dog has sensitive paws however, avoid stroking your hand down his leg to his feet.

**9.**

Perform Python Lifts on all of the legs during your session, although you do not need to work on them one after the other. Some dogs – even the best balanced - will find this work challenging; for many, the only time we touch their legs or feet is for unpleasant chores such as paw cleaning or nail clipping. Be patient and introduce the work slowly.

If you find that your dog fidgets or lifts his paw up, be tolerant: do not resist him by holding on to the foot or leg so that it becomes a battle, but instead gently go with the movement until he settles. You may find that doing some Raccoon TTouches first will help prepare him for this leg work.

*Note: If your dog has cruciate ligament problems, do not perform Python Lifts on the hind legs.*

### *SHOULDER ROCKING TTOUCH*

This TTouch can be invaluable if your dog finds it

hard to balance in the car and suffers from motion sickness, as it helps to teach him how to transfer his body weight from side to side, redistributing it from one foot to the other.

(photo: Toni Shelbourne)

**1.**
Lightly place one hand, palm down, on top of your dog's withers. If you are standing, position your feet a comfortable distance apart so you are in a good balance yourself.

Keep your knees flexed and hip, elbow, shoulder and wrist joints relaxed too.

**2.**

Gently and slowly move your dog's withers away from you. Be very subtle and don't push your dog off balance – just sway his body very slightly sideways so he transfers his weight gradually from the foot closest to you to the one furthest away, without actually taking it off the ground.

Take care not to press down hard with your hand or use it to support yourself.

**3.**

Pause for a moment and then equally slowly and gently draw the withers towards you again. Repeat several times.

## *TELLINGTON TTOUCH BODY WRAPS*

In addition to the special TTouches, the Tellington TTouch system makes use of many different training aids. One of the most recognizable of these are the body wraps; employing stretchy bandages, these can be very successful with dogs that suffer from various travelling issues.

They influence the tactile part of the sensory system and can help dogs to settle and calm. Similarly, many people with autism find that gentle pressure helps to relieve feelings of anxiety. Think of it as being a portable hug if you like - but whatever the reason why it works, the constant gentle pressure does appear to have a calming effect on the nervous system, providing reassurance and comfort if your dog is fearful or hyperactive.

Another advantage of wearing a body wrap is that it produces an increased awareness of posture, with a consequent improvement in co-ordination and balance. This can be of immense benefit to dogs who suffer from motion sickness and who find it difficult to settle due to the constant movement of the car. Wraps can also be invaluable in overcoming fears of containment, so if you are thinking of using a car seatbelt harness but your dog has never worn one before, the body wrap can be a great intermediate step in teaching him to be comfortable about it.

It is important that the bandage you use is stretchy, as this allows it to exert a light pressure which stays in constant contact with your dog's body as he moves, without restricting his movement. ACE wraps are ideal and come in a range of lengths and widths according to the size of your dog: if you have difficulty getting hold of them, they can be purchased from the UK Tellington TTouch Guild Office shop (see the Contacts & Resources section at the end). Alternatives include equine tail or exercise bandages sold in equestrian stores, or a crepe bandage if you can't get hold of anything else. Do not use Vetrap, as it is hard to undo quickly if necessary, and the hairs of long-coated dogs can get caught up in it.

Make sure there is plenty of give in the fabric; with time and use the stretchiness eventually becomes lost and the wrap will need replacing.

Introduce the wrap in familiar surroundings where your dog feels safe and relaxed. Only when he is completely accustomed to, and comfortable wearing it should you use it on him while doing any travel training or during journeys in the car.

If you find that a wrap doesn't seem to help much

on the first occasion that you use it, do persevere, and try using it in conjunction with the TTouches and ground work. Even if you find that a wrap or Thundershirt (see following section) used by itself helps a lot, it is still worthwhile also doing some TTouches, as this often enhances the effect even further, helping your dog to make positive, permanent changes. Both TTouches and Body Wraps have a cumulative effect, so use them regularly.

It is advisable to enlist the help of another person, who can do the driving the first few times you travel your dog while wearing a wrap, so that you are free to keep an eye on him. If this isn't feasible and you have to cope single-handedly, then let your dog wear the body wrap prior to the journey, but remove it before setting off, just in case it slips, as you do not want to risk him getting caught up in it and panicking or injuring himself.

Whether you have help or not, it is sensible to choose routes for your training drives along roads where it will be possible to quickly and safely pull over to the side and stop if there is a problem. For safety, we suggest that on journeys lasting more than a few minutes, or where you cannot see him (if he is in a crate for example) you use a Thundershirt or close-fitting doggy T-shirt rather than a wrap.

### The Half Wrap
Body wraps can be used in a variety of different configurations to help in resolving a wide number of issues, but initially you should start with a simple half wrap - you may find that for many dogs this is quite sufficient anyway.

Provided you introduce it properly, most dogs enjoy

wearing a wrap, but even if you think your pet looks a bit comical in it, don't laugh at him - dogs can be just as sensitive as people about being ridiculed.

**1.**

Approach your dog calmly with the wrap, and with it bundled up in your hand, let him sniff at, and take a good look at it. Do not rush this stage. Stroke it gently against his sides and chest. You can even use it to do some circular TTouches on his shoulders and chest. If he is anxious about approaching it, place the wrap on the floor and put treats on top of it for him to eat.

**2.**

Once your dog is quite happy around the wrap, unroll and pass the centre of the bandage around the front of his chest. Bring the ends up across the shoulders, up over his back and cross them over just above his shoulder blades.

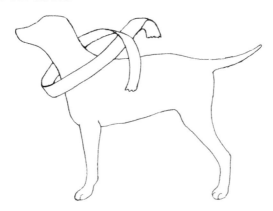

**3.**

Take both loose ends down the sides of his ribcage, behind the front legs. Cross them beneath his rib cage and bring them back up again over the top of his back.

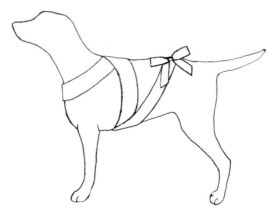

As you do this, keep the wrap close to his body and unravel it a little at a time from your hands so it doesn't flap around. Be careful not to inadvertently pull the ends too much at this stage, as some dogs may find this difficult to cope with. Try to be slow and smooth in your movements.

**4.**

Tie the ends in a bow or quick release knot so it can be quickly undone again if necessary. Make sure that the fastening lies off to one side of the spine, not directly on top of it. Alternatively, sew some Velcro to the bandage ends to secure it.

The wrap should be applied just firmly enough to keep it in place and enable it to maintain contact with the body – about the same sort of pressure as an elasticated tracksuit waistband. Check in various places to see if you can easily slide your hand beneath it. If it is too tight in one area and too loose in another, readjust it until the tension is the same throughout. Remember that its purpose is to provide feelings of security and sensory input, not to support, and it certainly shouldn't restrict movement or cause discomfort.

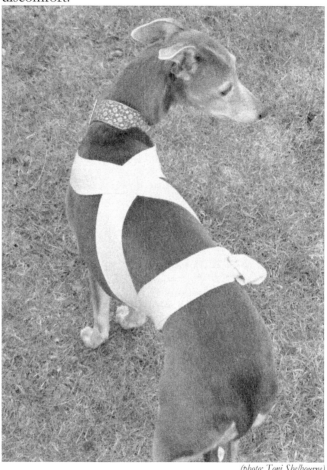

*(photo: Toni Shelbourne)*

**5.**

Encourage your dog to move while wearing the wrap: if he freezes use gentle coaxing, offer a really tasty treat or invite a gentle game with a favourite toy to overcome his reluctance. If he rubs or grabs at it, try to distract him. If after a few minutes he is still worrying at it, remove it and try again on another day. Before applying the wrap again, do more TTouches on him by way of preparation for wearing it.

**6.**

Even if your dog seems comfortable the first time he wears a wrap, remove it after a few minutes, and over the next few sessions gradually increase the duration it is worn for. On the build-up to working in and around the car and whilst travel training, leave the wrap on for a maximum of around twenty minutes before removing it; on the days you travel it can be worn for longer periods, and if safe to do so, for the whole journey.

Never leave your dog alone while he is wearing a wrap in case he gets caught up. Keep a close eye on him in case you need to make adjustments for comfort or safety, or if he wants it taken off. On very rare occasions some dogs appear to not tolerate body wraps at all. This may be down to an underlying health or pain issue so do consult your vet.

*You can find out more about using body wraps in 'All Wrapped Up For Pets: Improving function, performance and behaviour with Tellington TTouch Body Wraps' by Robyn Hood (see Contacts & Resources).*

## THUNDERSHIRT

In recent years various products have appeared on the market which can be used as an alternative to a body wrap. The best known of these is probably the Thundershirt, produced by a company which worked alongside Linda Tellington Jones in its development. The Thundershirt's comfortable, constant contact has a similar calming effect to a wrap, is easy to put on, and adjusts to fit different body shapes. If your dog tends to move around a lot in the car, if he is out of sight, or on journeys of more than a few minutes duration, a Thundershirt may be a safer option than a body wrap. Do, however, check that he doesn't overheat on warm days if you don't have air conditioning in your car.

*photo: Sarah Fisher)*

As when using wraps, a Thundershirt should be introduced carefully, breaking the process down into easy stages. It is secured using Velcro straps, and before fitting it, you should make sure that your dog is comfortable with the sound they make. Extra training and time may be required for dogs with hyper-noise sensitivity, especially if they are reactive to household noises such as frying food, bleeps on electrical equipment and the slamming of doors. Spend some time over a few sessions introducing the noise to him, but if the sound of the Velcro is just too much for him, we'd suggest that you stick with a body wrap or try using a close-fitting doggie T-shirt instead.

The first step in introducing the Thundershirt is to allow your dog to inspect it. Putting it on the floor and placing a few really tasty treats on top will encourage him to check it out and help in creating a positive association and overcoming any concerns he may have about it. Next, unfold it half way and lay it across his back for a few moments, offering a few more treats if necessary, as he gets used to the feeling.

If he is fine with this, open the Thundershirt up completely and put it on, closing the front fastening but leaving the side panels open. When your dog is happy about this, close the side panels to create a snug fit. As with using wraps, keep the initial introductory sessions and periods wearing it short; but once your dog is accustomed to wearing it, it can be left on for as long as required (weather permitting) although you should not leave him in it unsupervised.

## THE CONFIDENCE COURSE
### (Tellington TTouch Groundwork)

Balance (or lack of it) can play a huge part in how well (or poorly) your dog copes with the continually shifting environment of the car. Dogs with poor balance really struggle with their equilibrium, leading to anxiety, behavioural issues and nausea, so the more you can do to improve this aspect, the better. Many dogs are poorly balanced, although you might not be aware of the existence of your dog having issues in this respect unless you have problems such as pulling on the leash, which is frequently associated with it.

Ground work can be invaluable in helping to improve and refine balance. It is easy to set up a ground work

'Confidence Course' at home, using everyday objects to provide a variety of different surfaces and textures, and items that produce a slight movement underfoot. What might at first glance look like an obstacle course is actually exactly the opposite, with the aim being (as the name suggests) to promote confidence rather than to intentionally trip up, confuse or impede your dog. Working his way around the courses you set up will make him more aware of how he is moving, and help him to develop better balance, co-ordination and self-control. As well as having benefits for dogs who suffer from motion sickness, it is very useful in teaching Agility dogs to move more effortlessly and efficiently, and in helping dogs that pull on the leash to find better equilibrium physically and mentally. For older dogs it can be a great low-impact exercise to maintain flexibility and provide mental stimulation. A further bonus is that it's a great exercise for improving co-operation and communication between the two of you, and you will often find your powers of observation growing, and noticing the more subtle nuances in his posture, movement and expression.

You do not need lots of expensive equipment, but can easily improvise using objects you either already have to hand or can buy very cheaply.

*Examples of objects you might use* *(photo: Toni Shelbourne)*

Short lengths of plastic guttering, plastic plumbing pipes, foam pipe lagging or old broom handles make great poles which can be laid out on the ground for your dog to walk over. Slightly raise one or both ends of some poles by crushing an empty drink can in the centre to form a rest for the pole; or scatter them in a random 'pick up sticks' style pile which he has to pick his way through.

Use old bicycle tyres to similarly create mini-mazes to walk through. A short length of scaffold plank can be stepped over or walked along: raise one or both ends by placing a piece of half-profile plastic guttering beneath to create a low raised walkway. Use pieces of carpet, rubber bath mats, non-slip plastic and other materials to provide different textures and feels beneath his paws as he moves across them - you could even press the doormat from the front door into service! If you have a foam mattress from a garden lounger it will create a surface that yields slightly as he walks across it, giving yet another different experience; indoors you could use cushions from the sofa or old pillows from your bed.

Use plastic squash bottles weighted by half filling with water, or empty upturned plastic plant pots, or sports cones to create a slalom for your dog to weave in and out of. This is a great way of helping him learn how to transfer his weight from one foot to the other in order to balance. Co-ordination and stability problems tend to be greater if your dog is a bit one-sided, and this exercise will also help to even him up and increase his lateral suppleness.

Be inventive and imaginative – as long as the objects you choose are safe, you can create endless variations to keep your dog engaged. If you want to spend a little money and buy some equipment, look online for wobble cushions and physiotherapy equipment for dogs to add to your courses.

You can practice working over a Confidence Course indoors as well as outside; it is beneficial to vary the locations where you set it up, but start off by introducing it in an area where your dog feels safe and relaxed and there are few distractions.

*(photo: Sarah Fisher)*

Once you have a few pieces of equipment set up, pop a leash on your dog so you can help to guide him to each one in turn and can encourage him to slow down if he tries to rush. Attaching the leash to the collar can result in an inadvertent tug on his neck raising his head; this can then put him into a state of arousal or unbalance him and is exactly the opposite effect of the one you are trying to create. For preference, use a harness instead: and if it has a securely attached ring at the front of the chest, you can clip one end of a double-ended leash to it, and the other end of the leash to a ring at the top of the shoulders. The two points of contact this provides can allow you to be even more subtle in your communication with your dog – you can find out more about this from the Tellington TTouch online sites and books (see Contacts & Resources).

Ask your dog to approach and slowly move over, through or onto each of the obstacles in turn – it is not a race! If he rushes, he is more likely to become unbalanced and to make mistakes. Moving slowly encourages him to move with greater deliberation and precision, developing his physical control and self-restraint.

Vary the routes you take around the Confidence Course and the order and direction in which you approach each obstacle. Ask him to stop frequently, both in front of, while standing on, and after completing each piece of equipment, so he can collect himself physically, mentally and emotionally. Halting makes him more aware of his movements, encouraging him to focus his attention on the task in hand and to carefully plan his next move. If you need to give a little signal on the leash to encourage your dog to slow down or stop, remember to do so very gently, and to slowly allow the tension on it to go slack afterwards so you do not interfere with his balance. Remembering to allow this gentle release of tension on the leash is also important in helping to teach your dog to take responsibility for, and re-organise his equilibrium solely on his own initiative.

When your dog is negotiating your Confidence Courses with ease – and that means *only* when he is moving around them confidently, slowly and without rushing – try going round one a couple of times before starting any travel training sessions. If it is possible to set up a Confidence Course near your car, it can also have a positive effect on changing your dog's perception of the vehicle. With another focus (concentrating on working round the pieces of equipment) the presence of the scary car becomes more tolerable and together with the aid of reward based training, your dog can learn to be comfortable approaching it. Once calm and confident outside the car, your dog will be ready to take the next step of travel training within the car.

**You can see the Confidence Course being demonstrated online. Visit YouTube and search for 'Tellington TTouch for Dogs' and you will find plenty of video clips.**

# 5
# TRAVEL TRAINING

Travel training can play an important part in helping your dog to become a happy and confident passenger in the car; many of the modalities already suggested in the previous sections can provide support during the process, helping training to progress smoothly and successfully.

It is essential to chunk down travel training into little steps, and to move from one to the next at the pace dictated by your dog – don't expect to solve any issues he has within the space of a single session. With patience and by following a sensible plan you can, though, improve matters considerably and in many instances solve travelling problems completely. It is well worth investing the time and effort since not only will your dog benefit, but so will everyone else who has to share car space with him – and of course, it will be safer as well.

Because life does not always conveniently fit into the schedules and plans that you have made, there may however, be occasions when it is necessary to take your dog out in the car before you have completed your travel training programme.

If this happens, having a TTouch session with your dog earlier in the day will help him to relax, and create a calm frame of mind. You may also like to try one of the supporting modalities mentioned earlier; and the state of calm can be further enhanced through use of a body wrap or Thundershirt. These can be very useful aids both before travelling and during journeys. To maximize the effect of the Thundershirt or body wrap in the car, we suggest that your dog wears it regularly while at home with you, for short periods of around twenty minutes daily. If possible, arrange for someone else to drive, so that when the journey begins you can follow up the earlier TTouch session with a little more body work. Of course, if your dog is lying down quietly, then leave him alone and don't disturb him! If he does become agitated, some TTouch body work may help to quiet him, but only do it if it is safe for you to do so - do not put yourself or your dog at risk whilst travelling in a moving vehicle. Remember too, that legally, as well as for safety, you need to remain seat-belted in. Should you need to crate your dog for safety, or if you are on your own and have to do the driving yourself, then fit in a TTouch session with him before travelling, and once you arrive at your destination, you can calm and reassure him with some further work.

**Your new puppy's first journey**

Your new puppy's journey home with you can be traumatic if the breeder hasn't done any vehicle training with him. Unless carefully managed, this first trip can set him up for a whole host of future problems. Car travel may be an everyday occurrence for you, but consider it from a puppy's point of view: at eight weeks of age, with no warning and often no preparation, he is separated from his mother and littermates and then subjected to a fearful experience in the company of people he doesn't know and with whom he has not yet forged any bonds of trust.

Put in this context, it is easy to see why some dogs then really struggle to cope with successive car trips. It is therefore really important to try and make this first ride one which is as safe and as stress-free as possible. If possible, plan ahead and ask for an old towel to be placed in a sleeping place shared with his mother and siblings, and which you can take with you when you collect him. The familiar scents on it will help to comfort the puppy, both on the journey and when he reaches his new home, where it can be popped into his bed. If for some reason this isn't possible, try spraying some Adaptil onto a towel or blanket which can then be placed in the car.

When collecting your puppy, make sure you have another adult with you to drive. If your car is fitted with airbags, sit on the backseat with your puppy either on your lap, or in a small box held on your lap or by your side. As well as being the safest place for him, he is less liable to be a distraction to the driver. If possible, choose the most central part of the seat as it will be the most stable area, with least sideways motion. Do not allow children accompanying you to hold the puppy, no matter how excited they may be about the newest member of the family.

Before setting off, check that the puppy hasn't just eaten, and ensure that he has an opportunity to relieve himself. If he is awake, take the time to do some slow TTouch Ear Work. This will encourage calmness - possibly even sleep - and will help to settle a nervous puppy and counteract any possible nausea on this first journey. You can help him to feel physically and emotionally secure by wrapping him in a blanket, along with the smelly towel retrieved from his sleeping area, and containing him on your lap or in a small box.

A sturdy open-topped cardboard box is fine – but check that the bottom has been reinforced and will not drop out. Whether he is in a box or a special pet carrier, maintain physical contact with him at all times. If he wakes, is restless or whines during the journey, resume doing Ear Work. You can also do some of the circular TTouches such as the Clouded Leopard or Raccoon, described in the section on Tellington TTouch body work in Part 4 of this book. Remember to have plenty of fresh air circulating around the car but ensure that you keep him warm and do not allow him to become chilled by it, as puppies cannot regulate their body heat as efficiently as older dogs.

If you have a long journey, you may need to make several stops. Although you won't be able to put your puppy down on the ground at service stations, you will at least be able to give him a break from the noise and movement of the car. Do some more TTouches before moving off again.

Once at home, continue to work on travel training with him. Your first few journeys should not just be outings to the vets for vaccinations, as this could create negative associations with the car. Follow the stages listed in the section which follows, on confidence-building for anxious dogs. You may not need to go quite as slowly as for a nervous older dog, but it will ensure that your youngster considers the car to be a safe and comfortable place. Puppies can often suffer initially from motion sickness, and in this instance Ear Work can once again prove of benefit, used both before and during travel.

If you are collecting a dog from a rescue shelter, and aren't sure how he will cope, you can apply most of the same principles as with a puppy. While it might not be safe or appropriate to actually have him on your lap or sitting next to you, a little time spent on preparing him for the journey before setting off can help him to feel more confident as well as starting the bonding process with you.

## Building up confidence:
## Travel training for anxious dogs

If your dog is anxious in the car, the more preparation you can do prior to travel training, the better. This work can also be useful to do with a new puppy, helping to instil confidence from the start.

If your dog is really terrified of the car, maybe refusing even to go near it, try allowing a break of one or two weeks, and use this time to introduce some Tellington TTouch work and start any holistic remedies you want to try. When reintroducing your dog to vehicles, be aware that if he is very fearful, he may have an adrenalin boost each time you approach the car initially, so when training resumes, try working around the car every second or third day to allow time for stress hormones to leave his body.

Use whatever motivates your dog best to encourage and reward him and to help in developing pleasant associations with the car, whether it be food, toys, or a huge fuss from you. Don't be stingy with your rewards either! They can also provide a useful gauge as to how well he is coping: for example, if your normally food-loving dog won't touch treats when they are offered, then go back a stage in your training, as his anxiety level is too high for him to accept them. Periodically re-offer the treat; when he does take it, you'll know that his stress levels are abating.

When training in and around the car, increase the duration of each training session slowly – by just a few seconds at a time if necessary, and always try to finish earlier rather than later so you can end on a successful note. Bear in mind that when confronted for too long with a fearful situation, the over-exposure tends to result in anxiety levels escalating rather than lessening.

Where it is feasible to do so, using the TTouch body work and a body wrap or Thundershirt during each stage of training will often be beneficial; consider also using some of the various modalities discussed in Part 4 to help support him throughout travel training.

Always be aware of your own welfare if your dog is in a state of extreme fear, excitement or high arousal, as he may behave unpredictably at such times. Read through the notes on safety in the TTouch section, and if necessary, enlist the help of an experienced and knowledgeable trainer or practitioner.

### *Step 1:*

Perform regular ten to twenty minute TTouch body work sessions on your dog, teaching it at home in a place where you both feel comfortable and composed. Later, you can use it during each step of your travel training to help calm and relax your dog.

### *Step 2:*

Don't be in a rush to start working in the car itself. When you are confident in performing the TTouches, and your dog is enjoying the work, progress to simply working while in view of it. This may have to be at a fair distance if he has a high level of concern. Do just a few minutes of TTouch body work on him while near the car, then stop and go and do something else which is really fun and rewarding for your dog. Be sure to only spend a few moments in view of the car; remember that more is not necessarily better, and can actually be counter-productive. Far better to finish a session early on a positive note!

Use your treats and toys as a guide as to how close he can be and still positively interact with you and them. Try also setting up a few of the obstacles from a Tellington TTouch Confidence Course around or near the car to give him something else to focus on – but as with the TTouches, introduce it first on familiar home ground where he feels safe.

### *Step 3:*

When your dog is ready to start moving closer to the car, do so in very small stages – 30 cm (12 inches) at a time, or even less if necessary. Try scattering a few really tasty treats on the ground nearby; you could also try giving him his meals near to the car, gradually moving his bowl a little closer as his confidence grows, until finally it is next to it. Beware of moving it too close too soon as you do not want anxiety to cause him to bolt the food or take air in with it. Never lose sight of the fact that you are aiming to build confidence, not to increase stress levels; be patient and don't try to hurry the process. Your priority is to keep your dog calm, not to overwhelm him with the experience.

Don't assume that each time you start a session you will be able to begin at the same point as you left off during the previous one. Always commence at a distance your dog is very comfortable with, although you may find that during successive sessions he is able to progress more quickly to the closer distance. Do not force him to move closer, but be guided by his response: training should not be something you do *to* your dog, but something you do *with* him - he needs to feel safe at all times and to participate in the process. Actions which are achieved without duress are far more likely to be repeated!

At all times keep a close eye out for any indications that he is feeling stressed. If you think he may be, stop the session and continue again another time, as you do not want to pressurize him so much that it triggers a full blown fear response. Always give him the benefit of the doubt if you are not sure how to interpret what you are seeing, and seek help from an experienced trainer or practitioner.

Once your dog can move around the outside of the car confidently with the car doors shut, repeat the process with the car doors open. Have all the doors open; or if you don't have a driveway you can park on, then open all those closest to the pavement. Be prepared to start at the furthest distance again and take time to work up to walking near and around the car again. As before, do not rush this stage.

## *Step 4:*

Once your dog will happily walk up to and around the car, the next step is to ask him to get in it. This exercise is more difficult to set up if you don't have a secure enclosed gated driveway where you can park your car, but not impossible. Maybe a neighbour or friend might allow you to borrow theirs; or if you have a quiet car park, or safe open space situated away from nearby roads close to your house, perhaps you could set up training sessions there, walking your dog to the safe area. Other gated amenities may be available if you make enquiries locally.

For this stage, use a leash which is at least 2 metres long – or better still, a lightweight long line (available from online and high street retailers). A long line will make it easier for you to avoid inadvertently pulling at him if he suddenly tries to jump into, or out of the car. Wear a pair of driving or horse riding gloves to protect your hands from friction burns should your dog suddenly pull the line through your fingers. Rather than attaching the leash or long line to his collar, clip it onto an escape-proof harness, both to avoid accidental neck injury and to ensure your dog cannot back out of it should he become frightened.

*Step-in harness adapted to make it escape-proof*    *(photo: Toni Shelbourne)*

Do not use a retractable leash; it can be dangerous in such situations, as well as difficult for you to control with any finesse. If at all possible, enlist the help of a friend as an extra pair of hands may very well be needed. He or she must follow your instructions very carefully, so brief him or her in advance about their role.

Repeat all the earlier steps as usual, with the car engine switched off, and all the car doors open, including the boot door if it has one. Leaving the doors open will help to avoid him feeling trapped; and if he has an obvious exit, will increase the likelihood of him entering.

Use your dog's highest motivator, whether high value treats, or a favourite or new toy, to make the interior seem a more inviting place. Letting him see clearly what you are doing, place them just inside the car so he can easily reach in, grab them, and if he wants, to then retreat with them. Be encouraging, and be patient, as it may take him a moment or two to nerve himself to retrieve the goodies. If he finds it all too challenging, don't force matters, but instead go back to Steps 2 and 3 and spend a little more time building up his confidence and positive associations.

As he becomes bolder about taking a treat or toy from the car, you can gradually start to increase the distance he has to reach in to get them. Eventually he will have to actually step up into the car – at this point the motivator you use should be *really* high value. If he jumps onto the back seat and then wants to run straight through the car and out the other side initially, that's fine, but do be prepared for this possibility. Make sure that the long line is slack at all times and long enough that he can do this safely. This is why setting up the exercise in a safe location is important, and the assistance of a friend invaluable.

You may find that it helps to increase your dog's

confidence if you get in first, and then call him to you, showing him the treats or toy; this is, of course, when having an assistant is essential. Do not drag, push, pull or coerce your dog in any way, no matter how gently: make this stage enjoyable and setting foot inside the car entirely his choice.

As he grows more comfortable about jumping in and out of the car, try hiding the rewards so he has to spend more time in there finding them. Sit inside yourself, encouraging him to remain a little longer in there with you, offering treats or playing a brief, fun game with him. Keep things rewarding and unpressurized for him - heap on the praise and keep the sessions really short.

As his confidence develops, you can progress to closing the doors; at first you may need to be inside the car with him. Shut one door at a time (ask your assistant to do this for you) and as quietly as possible; leave the windows open slightly to minimise any pressure changes which might make him feel uncomfortable or anxious. Shut the door nearest to your dog last of all. Don't attempt too much too soon: as always, err on the side of caution, spreading the work out over several sessions and if at any time he shows concern, return to the previous stage which he was relaxed and confident about. Build up the length of time you are able to sit quietly together inside the car with the doors closed.

### Step 5:
If you will eventually want your dog to travel in a crate, then once you have reached this point, where he is confident and calm about sitting in the car with you, might be a good time to introduce it. Familiarise

him with it at home first of all (see Part 3) before transferring it to the car. Be prepared to go back a few steps in your training when first doing this and bear in mind that he may find being at a distance from you extremely challenging initially.

## *Step 6:*

Once your dog can jump into the car, lie down, receive treats and TTouch body work from you or play with a toy while all the car doors are shut without panicking or looking worried, you can then progress to starting the engine. If you have no-one to help, and have not introduced a travelling crate as in Step 5, you may first need to teach him to be confident about you being in the driver's seat while he is in a different part of the car.

Repeat *all* the earlier steps of the previous sessions. Only when your dog is comfortably settled and relaxed, try turning on the engine for a few seconds, and then turn it off again. The car should remain stationary at this point, so that your dog can simply become accustomed to the sound and vibration of the engine. Continue to use treats, toys and plenty of praise but try not to stare at your dog while observing him, or hold your breath at this stage as it might make him anxious. If he is mildly concerned, use a quiet but encouraging voice, increase the quality and rate of treats you hand out. Gradually increase the length of time the engine is running, until your dog can manage five to ten minutes without becoming stressed. Take as many sessions as necessary to build up to this.

## *Step 7:*

At this point, you will be ready to start moving the

car; you will need to arrange for someone else to do the driving so you are free to concentrate on your dog. If you judge that it is safe to do so, performing a few TTouches on him while the car is in motion may help to reassure and encourage calmness. If you have no-one to help you, then spend some time giving your dog a TTouch body work session beforehand. Make use too, of the Thundershirt and any holistic remedies you find helpful.

Initially, move the car only a metre or two, moving forward very slowly and smoothly, and braking again gently. This is often the stage that most people rush: do not be tempted to go for a mile, just because your dog has coped with moving a few yards. Coping is a start, but is not the same as being confident, which may take far longer to achieve. Be patient and take things slowly, increasing the time and distance over weeks, not days. If you see any visible signs of anxiety, end that session and take your progress a little more slowly.

Pick those routes with the fewest stops and starts or roundabouts at first, so your dog does not have too much movement within the car to contend with. If he is having trouble balancing or appears to suffer from motion sickness (bear in mind that vomiting may also be stress-related) try some of the suggestions in the previous chapters.

As your training progresses, driving your dog to a nearby park and having some fun before another short drive home may help to develop some favourable associations with car journeys. It also means that if you have misjudged your dog's confidence levels and he refuses to get back in the car, it won't be too far for you to walk him home and retrieve your car later.

After finishing each short training session, use some

more TTouch body work to help diminish any residual anxiety your dog may be feeling, and so that you end on a calm note.

## Dogs anxious about the car boot door being closed
If you are a dog, then having a large object come swinging down on you whilst in a confined space can be very scary! Like us, dogs can suffer from claustrophobia, and in such a situation may cower, bark hysterically, spin, bite at the boot door, or even at you.

Quite apart from often being far too tight a space for your dog to travel in comfortably (particularly in small family hatchbacks), placing him in the rear cargo section of a car is inadvisable anyway, as it is not a safe place for him to be. In the event of an accident, the front of the vehicle and the rear boot zone are designed to absorb impact by crumpling as one of the ways of protecting the driver and passengers within the car cabin: think crushed soda can and you'll get the general idea.

For preference, travel your dog on the back seat; or if you prefer and the rear seats aren't fixed, fold them down flat; this will still enable your dog to still ride safely within the protected area of the car while giving him a little more space and a more level surface.

If you need to load him into the car via the rear door, the lowered seats will allow him room to retreat away from it, but if even so, he still has concerns about it being shut, then you'll need to spend some time on training. If his anxieties are low to moderate, working on the issue will prevent it from escalating and save you both a lot of future distress; a suggested plan of action is included below. If his concerns are moderate to high and especially if he shows any signs of aggression or there is any possibility of him injuring you or himself, then we would urge you to seek some professional help - it is likely that you will require experienced assistance to resolve the problem safely as well as successfully.

**Rear car door training**
Prepare your dog for success by doing TTouch body work and using a body wrap or Thundershirt before and during training sessions in or around the car. Break the car boot lid training down into lots of tiny steps, with each training session being very brief, just a few minutes in duration.

If your dog reacts negatively at any point, go back a stage in training, to a step where he is able to be calm and focused. Use a harness and a leash at least two metres (six feet) long. Should he attempt to leap out, you will then be able to ensure he doesn't dash into danger, but will still be able to allow him the freedom to move deeper into the car interior, away from the boot door, if he wishes. Attaching the leash to the harness instead of the collar will prevent any accidental injury to his neck if he does suddenly leap away.

Giving your dog choices is important; if he feels he can move away from whatever is making him feel anxious it will help him to feel calmer, and more able to deal with events he finds challenging.

### *Step 1:*
With your dog on a slack long leash attached to the harness, ask him for a sit/stay or down/stay while inside the car with the boot door fully open. Do not move on to the next stage until he is able to manage this; the ability to listen to you, and/or take a treat indicates your dog is feeling relaxed and able to learn.

By all means use a tasty treat to help lure him into the sit or down position as well as to reward him, but do not physically enforce it – remain hands off, and be patient if at first he cannot maintain it for long and immediately springs back to his feet again. This is a reflection of the depth of his anxiety rather than being 'disobedience' so do not reprimand him!

## *Step 2:*

The next step is to begin creating a positive association about you touching the boot door. Slowly reach up to touch the door handle with one hand, and with the other, simultaneously give your dog a treat, a fuss or whatever motivates him the most. If he looks a little worried but is staying still, give multiple treats one at a time in quick succession to promote the idea that this is a good place to be.

If being in the car is too much for him while you do this, try again but with him outside the car instead: with him on a slack long leash, ask him to sit while you touch the boot door.

If he is unable to manage even this, don't insist on it as he may need to be further away from the car in order to cope. This is where a long training line will come in handy, as it will enable you to be near the car while allowing him to stay at a distance he feels safe at. You can always throw a treat to him – but whatever the distance, remember that you will need to use very high value rewards.

Don't tell your dog off if he cannot cope; if he becomes anxious or distressed, he is telling you that the situation is too hard or over-stimulating. At the first signs of concern, take him away from the car and allow him to calm down. Ignoring such indicators may lead to your dog going into a full-blown fear reaction.

Help your dog to be successful by taking your time with this training, and do reward him lavishly with praise and/or another treat each time he maintains his composure. If you inadvertently misjudge matters and he does react negatively, stop the session for the time being, and consider seeking professional help from an experienced trainer.

If your dog is coping well, you can repeat the whole process of touching the boot door while it is in the fully open position several times, whilst you mark the behaviour with treats and praise.

At this stage you may have to give rapid reinforcement, so keep those treats coming! Observe your dog carefully and if his anxiety doesn't decrease, stop and perhaps do some TTouch body work whilst he is still in the boot area with the lid up or just outside the car. This will not reinforce his fears, and may help to reduce his stress or hyperactivity.

Only work on this exercise for a few minutes each time. Once he is reliably remaining calm (preferably in a sit/stay or down/stay), you can begin to gradually increase the length of time he can sustain this for by withholding the treat for a little longer, and increasing the length of time you are touching the door for a second at a time. This may seem very short to you, but for a fearful dog it will feel much longer!

*Do not move on to the next stage until your dog is completely comfortable with these two steps, and is confident and calm enough to listen to you and respond to sit/stay or down/stay while you touch the boot lid. As a safety measure always do the training with him on leash.*

## *Step 3:*

Once your dog is calm and confident about you touching the car boot lid, very slowly move it downwards by a tiny amount – two or three centimetres (one inch) – and then pause, and reward any calm behaviour. Again, you may at first need to be rapid with those rewards and give multiple treats. If moving the lid just a fraction proves too much for your dog however, *slowly* let the lid up again and remove your hand from it. Even if he appears to be calm it can be a good idea to allow the lid to fully open again anyway, as this will give him a few moments to breathe and calm down again. It will also stop you from getting over enthusiastic, rushing the process, and possibly missing vital signs from your dog.

He should still be on a slack long leash during this stage, as a safety precaution in case he jumps out. If this does happen, don't tell him off or try to stop him, just go back a stage in your training. Body language can sometimes be extremely subtle, not always easy to notice or correctly interpret, and it may be that your dog is not as confident about the earlier work as you thought and is not yet ready to progress further. Go back and repeat the earlier steps and if necessary, enlist the assistance of a good trainer or TTouch practitioner who can help you to 'read' your dog more accurately.

## *Step 4:*

Repeat this process until you can close the lid further and further without a reaction, taking it in very small stages each time. Beware of rushing the process, and during each session, always start off again from Step 1 rather than from the point you left off at in the previous session, so you can check on how your dog feels at this particular moment in time.

Reward often, and raise the lid back up regularly as well. This allows your dog a break from the stress of the training session, and gives you a chance to rest your arm and give your dog some more TTouches, a *gentle* game (you do not want him to get overexcited) or a big fuss, whichever you feel most appropriate. Keep each training session short, no more than a few minutes at a time, stopping early on a positive note rather than risking pushing your dog beyond his ability to cope and undoing all the good achieved so far.

## *Step 5:*

When you reach the point where you are ready to actually shut the boot door completely, do so slowly and softly, rather than slamming it. Make sure that you have first opened a side window so as to equalise the air pressure inside the car. You can reward this final stage by scattering a handful of treats in the boot just as you close it and by using vocal praise. If he remains calm, immediately open the boot again and reward with further praise and a bonus handful of treats.

If things don't go quite according to plan and your dog reacts negatively, open the door and quietly remove him from the car. In the next session go back to an earlier stage which he was very comfortable with, and use TTouch body work, body wraps and other modalities detailed in Part 3 to help support him through the training process.

**NB. You cannot do this training if your car has a self-closing boot. In this instance we suggest loading your dog from a side door, so that you can take immediate action if your dog panics.**

## Dogs that bark, are hyperactive in the car or lunge at things outside whilst travelling

Barking can rapidly raise your own stress levels, making it hard for you to behave calmly and not to react irritably – even though you know that if you shout at your dog it will only compound his behaviour. It can also be potentially dangerous, making it very difficult to concentrate on driving safely.

If your dog barks or jumps around in the car, you will need to tailor your approach according to the underlying cause: if it is due to anxiety, try the suggestions in the section on helping anxious and fearful dogs.

If he barks through sheer excitement and anticipation of going to a place he finds fun (such as the park) then spend some time changing his associations, and making the car, and everything you do in and around it an oasis of calm.

A few ideas you might like to try include:

- Give your dog a TTouch body work session and pop on a body wrap or Thundershirt before he gets in the car, so that he is feeling relaxed and mellow.
- Set up a Confidence Course around the car and work through it a few times, as with a nervous dog.
- Without making a fuss, put him in the car, and then quietly take him straight out again, and maybe do a few TTouches, or go round the Confidence Course again.
- Put him in the car with you while it is parked and do some more TTouch body work with him, listen to calm music, or read a book - anything that involves you being still and quiet.

- If he will eat while in the car, try offering him a Kong stuffed tightly with really tasty treats, to encourage him to settle quietly. Chewing and nibbling at it can also be a stress-relieving activity.
- Teach some Real Dog Yoga postures, expressions and actions to encourage him to relax.

Barking can be a really challenging behaviour for you to ignore; if it is due to excitement, and you are finding it difficult to remain calm and soothing, try wearing ear plugs if necessary to help muffle the noise while working through the above suggestions in a stationary car (but not while driving).

You can use these quiet activities to give you, as well as your dog, a different focus and make it easier for you to ignore your dog's unwanted behaviour while still being close enough to him to reward calm behaviour with treats or *calm* praise (as you do not want to excite him) when he presents it. It can be very helpful to spend some time teaching clicker training to your dog, as this will make it easy for you to mark those moments where he is quiet, which with some dogs may only be very brief initially.

The next stages are similar to those taken with an anxious dog: sitting in the car with the engine running, then moving a few feet, then a short distance. If the problem only occurs when you are on the move, ask a friend to help out by driving while you do some TTouches with him. Once you have achieved your goal, remember to continue to take your dog regularly for 'boring' drives, not always to the park or where something exciting happens when you reach your destination.

If your dog barks because he is aroused by things he

can see outside the car, or if he tries to lunge at them, then working to create confidence and calmness with those objects that create concern or anxiety will, of course, be a sensible move. This is usually best achieved through one-to-one sessions with a good trainer; such work is unlikely to be practicable within a class situation. In the meantime, remove the source of the issue by teaching him to go in a crate (see Part 3). Create calm, positive associations with it as already discussed, and in the case of wire crates, cover with a sheet on the window sides so there is no visual stimulus from objects outside.

Dogs that fly at the windows or bounce around the car interior shadow-chasing as the sunlight hits the floor around them may benefit from tinted glass or sun shades fitted to side and rear windows but may do better if crated as above, with a cover over the crate to eliminate the visual stimulus.

*

*All dogs are individuals; some will progress rapidly, others more slowly through the travel training exercises outlined here. In some cases, combining several supporting modalities alongside travel training may be necessary; read all the other sections in the book to find out more. Even if your dog has only mild travelling issues, it is worth considering using them anyway, as it will enable you to produce quicker and more effective results than if following the travel training steps on their own.*

*There are also other creative ways in addition to those we have suggested here that can help in building a positive association with the car and travelling, but which need a little more skill and knowledge to achieve. To find out more about these: or if fears are very deeply entrenched: or if you are struggling to apply any of the suggestions made in this book: or simply need an extra pair of hands to help out, we recommend contacting a local, experienced, reward-based trainer or a Tellington TTouch practitioner. You may find it helpful to do this in any case during the initial work in and around your car.*

# FURTHER READING

**Getting in TTouch with Your Dog: A gentle approach to influencing behaviour, health and performance** by Linda Tellington-Jones *(Quiller Publishing)*

**All Wrapped up for Pets: Improving function, performance and behaviour with Tellington TTouch Body Wraps** by Robyn Hood *(available from TTEAM offices – see below for contact details)*

**Unlock Your Dog's Potential: How to achieve a calm and happy canine** by Sarah Fisher *(David & Charles)*

**100 Ways to Train the Perfect Dog** by Sarah Fisher and Marie Miller *(David & Charles)*

**100 Ways to Solve Your Dog's Problems** by Sarah Fisher and Marie Miller *(David & Charles)*

**The Holistic Dog: A Complete Guide to Natural Health Care** by Holly Mash *(Crowood Press)*

**Essential Care for Dogs: A Holistic Way of Life** by Jackie Drakeford and Mark Elliott MRCVS *(Swan Hill Press)*

**Bach Flower Remedies for Dogs** by Martin J Scott and Gael Mariani *(Findhorn Press)*

**On Talking Terms With Dogs** by Turid Rugaas *(First Stone)*

**Clicker Training for Dogs** by Karen Pryor *(Sunshine Books)*

**The Truth about Wolves and Dogs** by Toni Shelbourne *(Hubble & Hattie)*

**Canine Behaviour: A Photo Illustrated Handbook** by Barbara Handelman *(First Stone)*

**Homeopathic Care for Cats and Dogs** by Don Hamilton, DVM *(North Atlantic Books)*

**Walking the dog: Motorway walks for drivers and dogs** by Lezli Rees *(Veloce Publishing Ltd)*

**Help Your Dog Heal Itself: Insights into Hidden Problems Through the Aromatic Language of Dogs** by Caroline Ingraham *(Ingraham Trading Ltd)*

**Acu-Dog: A Guide to Canine Acupressure by** Amy Snow & Nancy Zidonis *(Tallgrass Publishing)*

**Real Dog Yoga** by Jo-Rosie Haffenden *(The Pet Book Publishing Company)*

# CONTACTS & RESOURCES

*The references provided in this section are for informational purposes only and do not constitute endorsement of any sources or products. Readers should be aware that the websites listed in this book may change.*

## ACUPRESSURE
Tallgrass Animal Acupressure Institute
*Details of training courses, workshops and a list of practitioners at:*
**www.tallgrasspublishers.com**
*See also Further Reading*

## ADAPTIL
*Available from vets, pet shops and online.*
**www.adaptil.co.uk**

## APPLIED ZOOPHARMACOGNOSY
*Case studies, training, and a list of practitioners can be found at:*
**www.ingraham.co.uk**
*See also Further Reading*

## BACH FLOWER REMEDIES
**www.bachcentre.com**
**www.bachfloweressences.co.uk**
**www.bachflowerpets.com**
*As well as the original Bach remedies there are other companies which produce flower remedies, and have even expanded on the original 38*

*remedies – for preference look for alcohol-free versions.*
*See also Further Reading*

## CLICKER TRAINING
**www.clickertraining.com**

## CONFIDENCE COURSE EQUIPMENT
If you would like to buy equipment specially designed for dogs, you may find this a useful source:
**http://www.activebalance-vetphysio.co.uk/**

## ESCAPE PROOF HARNESSES
*We recommend that you avoid any harnesses which tighten around the dog's body. You may be able to find a friendly local saddler who will adapt an existing step-in harness for you to make it escape-proof, or alternatively you can buy either an off-the-peg or made-to-measure one.*
Indi Dog
Range of harnesses: look for the escape-proof "Houdini Harness"
**http://www.indi-dog.co.uk/**

Ruffwear
**www.ruffwear.co.uk**
**and www.ruffwear.com**

## HERBALISM
British Association of Veterinary Herbalists
**www.herbalvets.org.uk**

## HOMEOPATHY
British Association of Homeopathic Veterinary Surgeons
**www.bahvs.com**
*See also Further Reading*

## LAW
*UK law with regard to controlling your dog in public places:*

https://www.gov.uk/control-dog-public/overview

The Highway Code:
https://www.gov.uk/guidance/the-highway-code
**MUSIC**
Through a Dogs Ear
**http://throughadogsear.com**

## PET BEHAVIOUR COUNSELLORS
Association of Pet Behaviour Counsellors
**www.apbc.org.uk**

## PHYSIOTHERAPISTS
Association of Chartered Physiotherapists in Animal Therapy
**www.acpat.org**

McTimoney Chiropractic
**www.mctimoneychiropractic.org**
**www.mctimoney-animal.org.uk**

Bowen Technique
**www.bowen-technique.co.uk**

## TELLINGTON TTOUCH TRAINING
*For further information about Tellington TTouch, equipment (including harnesses, wraps and Thundershirts), books, DVDs and links to online videos or to contact a Tellington TTouch practitioner visit the following TTouch websites.*
*See also Further Reading.*

TTouch Australia
**www.listeningtowhispers.com**

TTouch Austria
**www.tteam.at**

Tellington TTouch Canada
5435 Rochdell Road
Vernon, B.C. V1B 3E8
**www.tteam-ttouch.ca**

TTouch Germany
**www.tteam.de**

TTouch Ireland
**www.ttouchtteam-ireland.com**

TTouch Italy
**www.tteam.it**

TTouch Japan
**www.ttouch.jp**

TTouch Netherlands
**www.tteam-ttouch.nl**

TTouch New Zealand
**www.listeningtowhispers.com**

Tellington TTouch South Africa
**www.ttouchsa.co.za**

TTouch Switzerland
**www.tellingtonttouch.ch**

Tellington TTouch UK
Tilley Farm
Bath BA2 0AB
Tel: 01761 471182
**www.ttouchtteam.co.uk**

Tellington TTouch USA
1713 State Road 502

Santa Fe, NM 87506
**www.ttouch.com**

*You can watch the Tellington TTouches, body wraps and confidence course being demonstrated online: visit YouTube and search for 'Tellington TTouch for Dogs' and you will find plenty of video clips!*

*Tellington TTouch is also on Facebook at:* **Tellington TTouch Training Club** *and* **Tellington TTouch World**

## THUNDERSHIRTS
*Available from Tellington TTouch office: see above*

## TRAINING
Association of Pet Dog Trainers
**www.apdt.co.uk**

## MISCELLANEOUS
Motorway service stations
*Includes reviews of dog friendliness*
**www.motorwayservices.info**

Dog friendly pubs
*Places where you and your dog can take a break during journeys*
**www.doggiepubs.org.uk**

# NOTES

## MEDICATION:
Various drugs are available from your vet that may help with travel issues such as vomiting and anxiety. Some are not suitable for long term use and many have a long list of side effects, so in some cases you may find that by using them you are simply swopping one problem for another. The NOAH Compendium of Animal Medicines is a useful online resource for finding out more about known contra-indications and side effects of the various products available. Search by either product name or active ingredient at: www.noahcompendium.co.uk

## MUSIC
### Research studies on the effects of music on dogs:
Wells, D. L., et al. "The Influence of Auditory Stimulation on the Behaviour of Dogs Housed in a Rescue Shelter." *Animal Welfare 11 (2002): 385-393*

Wagner, S., et al. *BioAcoustic Research & Development Canine Research Summary* (2004)

You can read more about the effects of bioacoustics music and listen to samples on the website at Through a Dog's Ear: http://throughadogsear.com

## HERBAL PREPARATIONS
**Valerian:** www.petnutritioninfo.com/valerian-root-

benefits.html

**Hops:** www.petpoisonhelpline.com/poison/hops/

**Ginger:** Many claims have been made for the benefits of
ginger, and you may find the following of interest:
http://www.dogcancerblog.com/blog/ginger-to-help-
dogs-with-cancer/
http://www.whatisaginger.com/the-significance-of-ginger-
for-dogs/
http://www.drugs.com/npp/ginger.html


Find out more about other Help! Books on Facebook at
**Canine Ebooks by Toni Shelbourne and Karen Bush**

And on our website at
**http://tonishelbourneandkarenbush.jimdo.com/**

# ABOUT THE AUTHORS

## Toni Shelbourne

Born into a family mad about animals it seemed only natural that Toni would be destined for a career with them; she says 'animals just walked into our lives, sometimes arriving injured, others just flying in the window'.

She has worked with dogs and wild canids since the late 1980's; during a long and successful career with the Guide Dogs for the Blind Association she quickly progressed from kennel staff to supervisor and then to staff training. In 1997 she studied under Linda Tellington-Jones and other top Tellington TTouch Instructors, becoming one of the first pupils to qualify as a Companion Animal Practitioner in the UK. In 2000 she left GDBA to pursue her passion for the Tellington TTouch Method and is now one of the highest qualified practitioners in the UK, working with all animals including dogs, cats, small animals, birds, reptiles, wild life and non-domesticated animals.

In 2001, Toni joined the UK Wolf Conservation Trust, where she went on to become a Senior Wolf Handler and Education Officer for the organisation. Through observing the wolves at close quarters, Toni developed a unique insight into their behaviour which led her to question the prevailing popular ideas about the alpha theory in dogs – ideas which often came into direct conflict with her own knowledge and observations gained at first-hand.

In addition to her background in animal welfare and conservation issues, Toni edited the UK Wolf Conservation Trust's international magazine *Wolf Print* for two years, has contributed numerous features to national dog magazines, rescue society newsletters and websites and made many appearances on TV and radio. Her first book, *The Truth about Wolves & Dogs*, was published in 2012, and her second, *Among the Wolves: Memoirs of a Wolf Handler*, in 2015.

In 2015 Toni studied with Jo-Rosie Haffenden to become a Real Dog Yoga Instructor. This errorless learning method was featured on *Rescue Dogs to Super Dogs* and fits perfectly with TTouch.

As well as working privately with clients, Toni runs workshops, seminars, gives talks and demos and works closely with a number of rescue shelters and assistant dog organisations both with Tellington TTouch and Real Dog Yoga.

She also lectures on wolf behaviour and takes groups of people to interact with wolves at Wolf Watch UK.

**Email:**
ttouch1@btconnect.com
**Website:**
www.tonishelbourne.co.uk
**Facebook:**
The Truth about Wolves & Dogs
**Twitter:**
@tonishelbourne

## Karen Bush

Karen combines working with horses with writing about them and about her other great love, dogs. She has written hundreds of features which have appeared in leading national publications including *Horse & Rider*, *Your Horse*, *Pony*, *Horse & Pony*, *Horse*, and *Your Dog* and over twenty books including the best-selling *The Dog Expert*. Karen currently shares her home with two rescue whippets.

**Websites:**
www.karenbush.jimdo.com
www.dogfriendlygardening.jimdo.com
**Facebook:**
Dog friendly gardening


**Contact us at:**
**Website:**
http://tonishelbourneandkarenbush.jimdo.com
**Facebook:**
Canine Ebooks by Toni Shelbourne and Karen Bush

# INDEX

Printed in Great Britain
by Amazon